PARTY POLITICS & SOCIAL CLEAVAGES IN TURKEY

PARTY POLITICS &

SOCIAL CLEAVAGES

IN TURKEY

ERGUN ÖZBUDUN

LYNNE
RIENNER
PUBLISHERS

BOULDER
LONDON

Published in the United States of America in 2013 by
Lynne Rienner Publishers, Inc.
1800 30th Street, Boulder, Colorado 80301
www.rienner.com

and in the United Kingdom by
Lynne Rienner Publishers, Inc.
3 Henrietta Street, Covent Garden, London WC2E 8LU

Library of Congress Cataloging-in-Publication Data
Özbudun, Ergun.
  Party politics and social cleavages in Turkey / Ergun Özbudun.
    pages cm
  Includes bibliographical references and index.
  ISBN 978-1-58826-900-3 (alk. paper)
1. Political parties—Turkey. 2. Turkey—Politics and government—1960–
3. Social conflict—Turkey. I. Title.
  JQ1809.A795O93 2013
  324.2561—dc23
                                                              2012049139

British Cataloguing in Publication Data
A Cataloguing in Publication record for this book
is available from the British Library.

Printed and bound in the United States of America

The paper used in this publication meets the requirements
of the American National Standard for Permanence of
Paper for Printed Library Materials Z39.48-1992.

5 4 3 2 1

Contents

Tables

Acronyms and Abbreviations

AKP	Justice and Development Party
ANAP	Motherland Party
AP	Justice Party
BDP	Peace and Democracy Party
CGP	Republican Reliance Party
CHP	Republican People's Party
CKMP	Republican Peasant Nation Party
CMP	Republican Nation Party
CUP	Committee of Union and Progress
DEHAP	Democratic People's Party
DemP	Democratic Party
DEP	Democracy Party
DP	Democrat Party
DSP	Democratic Left Party
DTP	Democratic Society Party
DYP	True Path Party
EU	European Union
FP	Virtue Party
GeP	Young Party
GP	Reliance Party
HADEP	Democracy Party of the People

HEP	People's Labor Party
HF	People's Party
HP	Populist Party
HürP	Freedom Party
IDP	Reformist Democracy Party
KONDA	Public Opinion Research and Consultancy Company
MÇP	Nationalist Work Party
MDP	Nationalist Democracy Party
MHP	Nationalist Action Party
MNP	National Order Party
MP	Nation Party
MSP	National Salvation Party
NGOs	nongovernmental organizations
NSC	National Security Council
PKK	Kurdistan Workers' Party
RP	Welfare Party
SHP	Social Democratic Populist Party
SODEP	Social Democratic Party
SP	Felicity Party
TBP	Turkey's Unity Party
TCF	Progressive Republican Party
TESAV	Turkish Social, Economic, and Political Research Foundation
TİP	Turkish Labor Party
TÜSİAD	Turkish Association of Industrialists and Businessmen
YTP	New Turkey Party

Party Politics & Social Cleavages in Turkey

1

The Party System and Social Cleavages in Turkey

TURKEY PRESENTS AN INTERESTING CASE FOR THE COM-
parative study of political parties. It is a "second wave" democracy,[1] where multiparty competitive politics has been going on
since the mid-1940s, preceded by an authoritarian, single-party
system between 1925 and 1946.[2] Since 1946, the Turkish party
system has displayed many forms and characteristics. The period
between the transition to multiparty politics and the military intervention of 1960 was a textbook example of a two-party system.
The retransition to democracy in 1961, after a relatively short
period of military rule, led to a fragmentation of the party system,
or the proliferation of political parties. Thus, the period between
1961 and the military coup of 1980 can be characterized as a multiparty system displaying certain features of an "extreme" or
"polarized" system as described by Giovanni Sartori.[3]

With the semicompetitive elections of 1983 (see Chapter 3),
which ended the three-year period (1980–1983) of military government of the National Security Council (NSC) regime, the Motherland Party (ANAP) was able to win the absolute majority of the
National Assembly seats and to form a single-party government in
two consecutive elections (1983 and 1987). Thus, the number of
parties represented in parliament declined, partly due to the effects

1

of the 10 percent national electoral threshold introduced by the military regime. However, with the erosion of the ANAP's popular support starting from the 1991 elections, another period of extreme multipartyism emerged. This period also witnessed the rise of the Islamist-inspired Welfare Party (RP), which contributed to increased polarization in the party system. The end result of this polarization was the so-called postmodern coup of 28 February 1997, which forced the RP-led coalition government to resign, and the eventual banning of the RP by the Constitutional Court.

The 2002 parliamentary elections opened up a new page in the history of the Turkish party system. The Justice and Development Party (AKP; one of the successor parties to the RP) won an absolute majority of seats in parliament and formed a single-party government, the first since 1991. The AKP repeated this success in the 2007 and 2011 parliamentary elections, each time increasing its percentage of votes. Thus, at the moment, the AKP appears to be the predominant party, once again marking a transformation of the party system. The so-called three maladies of the Turkish party system (fragmentation, volatility, and polarization) will be analyzed in Chapter 4 as well as the recent trend toward a predominant party system.

If one reason for the changes in the party system is the increasing social and ideological diversification within Turkish society, another is a more external one; namely, the effects of military coups and the changes in the electoral system. Indeed, the military government of 1960–1961 closed down the ousted Democrat Party (DP), and the military regime of 1980–1983 banned all political parties that existed prior to the coup. Similarly, during the semimilitary regime of 1971–1973, the Islamist-leaning National Order Party (MNP) and the Marxist Turkish Labor Party (TİP) were closed down by the Constitutional Court. In the atmosphere created by the postmodern coup of 1997, the RP and its successor, the Virtue Party (FP), met the same fate.

The effects of electoral systems on party systems are well-known. Since the transition to multiparty politics, Turkey has tried a variety of electoral systems, from a simple plurality (first-past-the-post) system with party lists to many versions of proportional representation, such as the d'Hondt system (see Chapter 5) with or without a constituency threshold, the national remainder system, and finally a d'Hondt system with a 10 percent national threshold. The size of the constituencies also changed several times from relatively small (a maximum of six deputies) to quite large (a maximum of eighteen deputies). The effects of these changes are discussed in Chapter 5.

Since electoral systems strongly influence the distribution of seats in parliament, this has always been a hotly debated issue in Turkish politics. Thus, in Chapter 6, I address the current debates on the issue of electoral reform, the views of different political parties, and the studies carried out by various nongovernmental organizations (NGOs) and think tanks.

Beneath these apparently radical changes, however, the Turkish party system also displays a certain basic stability. In the sixteen truly free and competitive elections starting with that of 1950 (excluding the controversial elections of 1946), parties representing the conservative/liberal center-right tendency have always obtained a strong majority of votes under different names and under different electoral arrangements (see Chapter 3).[4] Such stability can be attributed, above all, to the enduring effects of the basic social cleavage in Turkey, described in this book as a center-periphery cleavage. Given the strong link between the cleavage structure and the party system both in general and in the Turkish case, I conclude the present chapter with a general and comparative analysis of the impact of social cleavages, and in Chapters 2 and 3 I analyze the historical roots of that impact and its persistence in the multiparty period. Throughout the book, the emphasis is on the party system rather than on individual parties. Even though the two areas often are inseparable, it remains true that "parties and party systems offer two quite distinct foci of analysis."[5] In the Turkish case, the system displays much greater persistence than parties.

Social Cleavages and Party Systems

Party systems reflect, to a greater or lesser degree, the social cleavage structure of societies. Cleavage structures influence various aspects of a party system. With regard to the number of parties, a society divided essentially by a single cleavage line is likely to give rise to a two-party system while a society with two distinct cleavage lines can be expected to produce a four-party system, and so forth.[6] The degree of intensity of the cleavages also affects an important dimension of the party system; namely, the degree of polarization, an important variable that distinguishes moderate and polarized multiparty systems.[7] In divided or segmented societies where cleavages follow racial, ethnic, linguistic, religious, or sectarian lines, the party system also displays characteristics quite different from those in more homogeneous societies. Clearly, the correspondence between cleavage structures and party systems is not a one-to-one relationship. Such relation may be stronger in some societies than in others.

Lipset and Rokkan's Model on Cleavage Structures and Party Systems

Seymour Martin Lipset and Stein Rokkan's seminal study on cleavage structures, party systems, and voter alignments[8] is probably the most influential and most often quoted work on the topic. Peter Mair rightly points out that their argument put forward "almost thirty years ago . . . even now continues to be one of the most familiar and most frequently cited theses within the field of comparative party studies."[9] The fundamental thesis of their work can be summarized in the following sentence: "The party systems of the 1960s reflect, with few but significant exceptions, the cleavage structure of the 1920s. . . . The party alternatives, and in remarkably many cases the party organizations, are older than the majorities of the national electorates."[10]

Lipset and Rokkan analyze the cleavage structures in Western democracies along two axes, territorial and functional. At one end of the territorial axis are "strictly local oppositions to encroachments of the aspiring or the dominant national elites and their bureaucracies: the typical reactions of peripheral regions, linguistic minorities, and culturally threatened populations to the pressures of the centralizing, standardizing, and 'rationalizing' machinery of the nation-state"; in other words, a center-periphery cleavage. Conflicts along the functional axis, on the other hand, *"cut across* the territorial units of the nation." They may be interest-specific oppositions and therefore amenable to rational bargaining, or ideological or "'friend-foe' oppositions of tight-knit religious or ideological movements . . . over conceptions of moral right and over the interpretations of history and human destiny."[11]

Applied to European party systems, these two axes have produced four dimensions of opposition in Western politics. Two of them were products of the national revolution and two of the Industrial Revolution. "In their basic characteristics of the party systems that emerged in the Western European politics during the early phase of competition and mobilization can be interpreted as products of *sequential interactions between these two fundamental processes of change.*"[12] The products of the national revolutions were those of center-periphery and church versus state. The first represented the opposition between the central, often bureaucratic, nation builders and the peripheral subject cultures. The second pitted the secular nation builders against the defenders of the corporate privileges of the Catholic Church. As Lipset and Rokkan argue, many "countries of Western Europe were all split to the core in the wake of the secularizing French Revolution and without exception developed strong parties for the defense of the Church, either explicitly as in Germany, the Low countries, Switzerland, Austria, Italy, and Spain or implicitly as in the case of the Right in France."[13]

The two other cleavages were the products of the Industrial Revolution. One was between rural and urban interests.

> The conflict between landed and urban interests was centered in the *commodity* market. The peasants wanted to sell their wares at the best possible prices and to buy what they needed from the industrial and urban producers at low cost. Such conflicts did not invariably prove party-forming. . . . Distinctly agrarian parties have only emerged where strong cultural oppositions have deepened and embittered the strictly economic conflicts.

The second also derived from the Industrial Revolution; the cleavage between the owners of capital and the working class, however, was much more pervasive. "Conflicts in the *labor* market proved much more uniformly divisive. Working-class parties emerged in every country of Europe in the wake of the early waves of industrialization."[14]

Lipset and Rokkan also argue that "sequential interactions between these two fundamental processes of change" constitute an important variable explaining the differences among Western European party systems, and that the differences are due to the

> first three of the four cleavage lines. . . . The "center-periphery," the church-state, and the land-industry cleavages generated national developments in *divergent* directions, while the owner-worker cleavage tended to bring the party systems *closer to each other* in their basic structure. The crucial differences among the party systems emerged in the early phases of competitive politics, before the final phase of mass mobilization. They reflected basic contrasts in the conditions and sequences of nation-building and in the structure of the economy at the point of take-off toward sustained growth.[15]

The Lipset and Rokkan model convincingly explains the formation of the Western European party systems and the differences among them due to the different sequential interactions in their early phases of competitive politics. This model also fits the Turkish case, as I analyze in detail in the chapters that follow, even though Turkey is not among the countries studied by Lipset and Rokkan. Indeed, in Turkey, too, the currently dominant cleavages (center-periphery and church-state) are the products of the national (nation building) revolution, and these two cleavages have often overlapped. The basic difference from Western European politics is that in Turkey, as in other Muslim-majority countries, there is no equivalent of the Catholic Church, with its autonomous structure and corporate privileges. However, a functionally similar cleavage developed between the ardent secularizers and the devout Muslims, combined with the center-periphery cleavage. On the other hand, as a late industrializing country, Turkey did not face the two cleavages that were the products of the Industrial Revolution. A distinctly agrarian party never appeared on the scene, and the capital owners–working class cleavage has remained of clearly secondary importance to the present day.

The heated academic debate on the Lipset-Rokkan thesis centers mostly on their "freezing hypothesis." Writing in the 1960s, they argued that the cleavage structures in the 1920s, more precisely at the time of the introduction of universal manhood suffrage, were essentially "frozen" since then. Thus, they claimed, "the parties which were able to establish mass organizations and entrench themselves in the local government structures before the final drive toward maximal mobilization have proved the most viable. The narrowing of the 'support market' brought about through the growth of mass parties during this final thrust toward full-suffrage democracy clearly left very few openings for new movements."[16]

The freezing hypothesis, however, has been challenged on several grounds. One point of view is that Lipset and Rokkan's observations were valid for the 1960s, but that they no longer are. Thus, Ivor Crewe argues that, since the 1940s, unprecedented levels of economic growth and welfare, "sustained peace on the European Continent, a vast expansion of higher education and increased travel and communication between countries combined to inculcate a new set of 'post-materialist' values in the younger generation—especially its better and more prosperous members."[17] Indeed, since Ronald Inglehart's influential book, students of electoral behavior have paid increasing attention to the rise of "postmaterialist" values and the emergence of new cleavages that cannot be properly explained under the fourfold typology of Lipset and Rokkan.

Among such postmaterialist concerns, one might cite environmentalism, quality of life, gender equality, identity issues, multiculturalism, participatory democracy, workplace democracy, and sexual freedom.[18] Thus, Inglehart, like many other scholars, concludes that

> to a considerable degree, Lipset and Rokkan were correct in speaking of a "freezing of party alignments" dating back to an era when modern, mass-party systems were established. Although

deep-rooted political party alignments continue to shape voting behavior in many countries, they no longer reflect the forces most likely to mobilize people to become politically active. Today the new axis of conflict is more apt to stimulate active protest and support for change than is the class-based axis that became institutionalized decades ago.[19]

A second group of scholars, using longer-term data from the 1920s and even going back to the nineteenth century, argue that the freeze hypothesis did not reflect realities even for the period before the 1970s. Such studies indicate that "not only does the recent volatility of the 1970s challenge the continued validity of the Lipset-Rokkan hypothesis, but the long-term analysis also suggests that the hypothesis never really carried much validity in the first place. Party systems have never been particularly stable, and hence the freeze has been exaggerated."[20]

Despite the accumulated results of these studies, however, Mair thinks that the critics of the Lipset-Rokkan thesis confuse the change in the aggregate support for individual parties with the persistence or change in the lines of cleavages. Thus, he argues that "there is no simple one-to-one correspondence between an individual party organization and the presence of a cleavage. . . . Thus while individual parties may rise and fall, the major 'alternatives' may therefore persist. . . . For while the various indices of aggregate electoral change may tell us a great deal about electoral stability/instability in general, they appear to tell us little about the persistence/decay of cleavages."[21]

While reaching a firm conclusion about this interesting debate is beyond the scope of the present study, it appears that what we now face is not only a change in the electoral fortunes of individual parties, but also changes in the cleavage structures. Certain conflicts that gave rise to older cleavages, such as those between the center and periphery and the church and state, were more or less solved as a result of modernization and democratization. The cleavage between urban and agrarian interests has never been of particular salience except in a limited number of countries. And the most pervasive of the four cleavages—namely, the one between the bourgeoisie and the working class—while still persistent in a majority of countries, has certainly lost much of its earlier intensity. Finally, new postmaterialist cleavages have emerged that cannot be subsumed under the four cleavages analyzed by Lipset and Rokkan.

Arend Lijphart identifies seven cleavage lines or "issue dimensions" in the twenty-one contemporary democracies that he studied. These are socioeconomic, religious, cultural-ethnic, urban-rural, regime support, foreign policy, and postmaterialism.[22] The first four correspond to Lipset and Rokkan's four cleavages. Thus, the socioeconomic dimension reflects the cleavage between the middle-class and working-class parties. Parties differ along this line with regard to their positions on four issues: "(1) government vs. private ownership of the means of production; (2) a strong vs. a weak governmental role in economic planning; (3) support of vs. opposition to the redistribution of wealth from the rich to the poor; and (4) the expansion of vs. resistance to governmental social welfare programs."[23] Lijphart argues that this dimension was of high salience in nineteen of the twenty-two democracies (the Fourth and the Fifth French Republic are listed separately), and of medium salience in only three of them (the United States, Canada, and Ireland). He concludes that, in none of these party systems, "the socioeconomic issue dimension is absent or of negligible importance."[24]

The religious dimension or the church-state cleavage is "the second most important dimension," and salient in half of the twenty-two democracies. Even though both religious and anti-clerical parties "have moderated their claims and counter claims to a large extent . . . the religious and secular parties are still divided on a range of moral issues, such as questions of marriage and divorce, birth control, abortion, sex education, pornography, and so on."[25]

With regard to the cultural-ethnic dimension, or the center-periphery cleavage in Lipset and Rokkan's terminology, Lijphart observes that it "appears much less frequently in the twenty-two party systems than the religious dimension, mainly because only four of our countries are ethnically and linguistically heterogeneous: Belgium, Canada, Switzerland and Finland."[26] However, this dimension is quite salient in a number of the newer, "third wave" democracies not included in his list of twenty-two democracies, such as Spain, Bulgaria, Romania, Latvia, Ukraine, Moldova, Macedonia, and Bosnia-Herzegovina. Ethnic conflicts even resulted in the fragmentation of the former Yugoslavia and the split of Czechoslavakia.

The remaining issue dimensions on Lijphart's list are of clearly minor salience nowadays. The agrarian parties in the Nordic countries "have tended to become less exclusively rural and to appeal to urban electorates too, prompted by the decline of the rural population."[27] The decline of the antisystem parties lessened the salience of the "regime support" dimension, just as the collapse of the Soviet Union and the European integration meant a convergence of political parties on foreign policy issues. Finally, "postmaterialism has not yet become the source of a new issue dimension in many party systems."[28]

While such comparative analyses provide highly valuable perspectives for the study of the party system and party system change in an individual country, they also demonstrate differences among them due to different patterns of national development, sequences, historical experiences, cultural specificities, and so on. This is also the case for Turkey. While, as pointed out above, Turkey partially fits the Lipset-Rokkan model in that the two currently prevailing cleavages (center-periphery and religion-secularism) are the products of the national revolution, many of its characteristics can be properly understood only in the light of its unique pattern of development.

Notes

1. On the waves of democratization, see Samuel P. Huntington, *The Third Wave: Democratization in the Late Twentieth Century* (Norman: University of Oklahoma Press, 1991).

2. On the Turkish single-party system, see Ergun Özbudun, "Established Revolution Versus Unfinished Revolution: Contrasting Patterns of Democratization in Mexico and Turkey," in Samuel P. Huntington and Clement H. Moore, eds., *Authoritarian Politics in Modern Society: The Dynamics of Established One-Party Systems* (New York: Basic Books, 1970), pp. 380–405; see also Ergun Özbudun, "The Nature of the Kemal-

ist Political Regime," in Ali Kazancıgil and Ergun Özbudun, eds., *Atatürk: Founder of a Modern State*, 2nd ed. (London: Hurst, 1997), pp. 79–102.

3. Giovanni Sartori, *Parties and Party Systems: A Framework for Analysis* (Cambridge: Cambridge University Press, 1976), pp. 131–173.

4. Ergun Özbudun, "Changes and Continuities in the Turkish Party System," *Representation* 42, no. 2 (2006): 129–137.

5. Peter Mair, *Party System Change: Approaches and Interpretations* (Oxford: Clarendon Press, 1997), p. 6.

6. Maurice Duverger, *Political Parties: Their Organization and Activity in the Modern State* (London: Methuen, 1959), pp. 231–234.

7. Sartori, *Parties and Party Systems,* pp. 135–136.

8. Seymour Martin Lipset and Stein Rokkan, "Cleavage Structures, Party Systems, and Voter Alignments: An Introduction," in Seymour Martin Lipset and Stein Rokkan, eds., *Party Systems and Voter Alignments: Cross-National Perspectives* (NewYork: Free Press, 1967), pp. 1–64.

9. Mair, *Party System Change,* p. 3.

10. Lipset and Rokkan, "Cleavage Structures," p. 50.

11. Ibid., pp. 10–11; emphasis in original.

12. Ibid., p. 34; emphasis in original.

13. Ibid., p. 34.

14. Ibid., p. 21; emphasis in original.

15. Ibid., p. 35; emphasis in original.

16. Ibid., p. 51; emphasis in original.

17. Ivor Crewe, "Introduction: Electoral Change in Western Democracies: A Framework for Analysis," in Ivor Crewe and David Denver, eds., *Electoral Change in Western Democracies: Patterns and Sources of Electoral Volatility* (London: Croom Helm, 1985), p. 5.

18. Ronald Inglehart, *The Silent Revolution: Changing Values and Political Styles Among Western Publics* (Princeton: Princeton University Press, 1977).

19. Ronald Inglehart, "The Changing Structure of Political Cleavages in Western Society," in Russell J. Dalton, Scott C. Flanagan, and Paul Allen Beck, eds., *Electoral Change in Advanced Industrial Democracies: Realignment or Dealignment?* (Princeton: Princeton University Press, 1984), p. 26; see also Scott C. Flanagan and Russell J. Dalton, "Parties Under Stress: Realignment and Dealignment in Advanced Industrial Societies," *West European Politics* 7, no. 1 (1984): 7–23. Flanagan and Dalton contend in the same vein that "throughout the postwar years the dominant partisan cleavage in most Western democracies distinguished between the working-class and bourgeois parties. Recently,

however, there have been increasing signs that this dominant class cleavage may also be moving into eclipse" (p. 10).

20. Mair, *Party System Change,* p. 62. Mair provides an excellent analysis of the debates over the freezing hypothesis (pp. 56–66). See also Svante Ersson and Jan-Erik Lane, "Democratic Party Systems in Europe: Dimensions, Change and Stability," *Scandinavian Political Studies* 5, no. 1 (1982): 67–96; Michal Shamir, "Are Western Party Systems Frozen?" *Comparative Political Studies* 17, no. 1 (1984): 35–79.

21. Mair, *Party System Change,* pp. 65–66.

22. Arend Lijphart, *Democracies: Patterns of Majoritarian and Consensus Government in Twenty-one Countries* (New Haven: Yale University Press, 1984), p. 128.

23. Ibid., p. 129.

24. Ibid., p. 132.

25. Ibid., pp. 132–135.

26. Ibid., p. 135.

27. Ibid., p. 136.

28. Ibid., p.140.

2

The Historical Roots of the Turkish Party System

SINCE ŞERIF MARDIN'S SEMINAL 1973 ARTICLE ENTITLED
"Center-Periphery Relations: A Key to Turkish Politics?,"[1] it is
generally accepted that the key social cleavage that has shaped the
Turkish party system is a center-periphery one. Mardin argues that
"the confrontation between center and periphery was the most
important social cleavage underlying Turkish politics and one that
seemed to have survived more than a century of modernization."[2]
However, he uses the terms "center" and "periphery" less in a
geographical than in a cultural sense. Thus, he argues,

> The state's claim to political and economic control was bol-
> stered by its title to cultural preeminence. Relative to the het-
> erogeneity of the periphery, the ruling class was singularly
> compact; this was, above all, a cultural phenomenon. Two ele-
> ments, one positive, one negative, may be isolated here. On the
> one hand, the entire mechanism of the state was permeated by
> the myth of the majesty of the Sultan; on the other hand, there
> were restrictions placed on the common mortal's access to the
> symbols of official culture. For much of the population, nomad
> or settled, rural or urban, this cultural separation was the most
> striking feature of the existence on the periphery. Rulers and

officials were heavily influenced in the cities by the culture of earlier, successful urban cultures such as the Iranian. . . . Not surprisingly, the periphery developed its own extremely varied counter-culture, but it was well-aware of its secondary cultural status. . . . This was particularly true of the lower classes, both rural and urban, for in this matter the urban masses could also be counted as part of the periphery.[3]

Clearly, Mardin equates the center with the state machinery, or the ruling class. In this sense, the *center-periphery cleavage* can be defined as one between the rulers and the ruled. Halil İnalcık, a leading Turkish historian, points to the sharpness of this dichotomy in the Ottoman Empire:

Ottoman society was divided into two major classes. The first one, called *askerî,* literally the "military," included those to whom the sultan had delegated religious or executive power through an imperial diploma, namely, officers of the court and the army, civil servants, and *ulema.* The second included the *reaya,* comprising all Muslim and non-Muslim subjects who paid taxes but had no part in the government. It was a fundamental rule of the empire to exclude its subjects from the privileges of the "military." . . . It was, in fine, the sultan's will alone that decided a man's status in society.[4]

Both statements attest to the essentially cultural character of the center-periphery cleavage in the Ottoman-Turkish context. Thus, these terms are used differently from the more geographical connotations in which Seymour Martin Lipset and Stein Rokkan use them (see Chapter 1). For example, small merchants and artisans are considered part of the periphery even if they reside in urban areas. On the other hand, even in the Turkish context, these terms are not entirely devoid of territorial or geographical connotations. During the time of the Ottoman Empire, the center of the statist or "high" culture was clearly Istanbul and, to a much lesser extent, the other large cities in the empire, whereas the peripheral culture was predominant in the rural areas and small towns of the provinces.

A division between the rulers and the ruled is certainly not peculiar to the Ottoman Empire; it can be observed in many countries, especially in the earlier phases of political modernization. However, it was particularly deep and long-lasting in the Ottoman-Turkish politics, and its causes must be found in certain special characteristics of the Ottoman Empire.

Obviously, a full analysis of these characteristics is beyond the scope of the present study.[5] However, a few points of comparison between Western European feudalism and the Ottoman state system are in order. Indeed, the fundamental differences between the two have attracted the attention of many classical and modern writers such as Niccolò Machiavelli, Jean Bodin, François Bernie, Charles Montesquieu, and Karl Marx. Machiavelli, for example, observes that "the entire Turkish empire is ruled by one master, and all other men are his servants; he divides his kingdom into *sandjaks* and dispatches various administrators to govern them, whom he transfers and changes at his pleasure . . . they are all slaves, bounded to him."[6]

The excessive concentration of authority in the sultans was due to several factors. First, in contrast to the medieval Western European feudalism, the Ottoman state did not have a hereditary nobility or an aristocratic class. The *sipahis* (fief holders) were essentially the servants of the state rather than members of a local nobility. The Ottoman system vested in the state the original ownership of all land, and limited the rights of the *sipahis* to the collection of the taxes and the supervision of peasants under their jurisdiction. The *sipahis'* source of livelihood was derived from the taxes they collected from the peasantry. In return for their land grant, they were expected to recruit, train, and support a local contingent of soldiers to join the imperial army in time of war. Again significantly for the present study, the fiefs (lands) were granted by the central government and, if necessary, could be taken away, although in normal circumstances they passed to the sons of the fief holders. Thus, H. A. R. Gibb and Harold Bowen observe that "the Ottoman feudal system seems to have differed from that of Western Europe chiefly in that the principal feudatories held their lands temporarily, in virtue of their offices. . . .

Hence the monarchy was exposed to little danger from the rivalry of this class of its tenants-in-chief."[7]

Another feature of the Ottoman state system that reinforced the rigid dichotomy between the ruler and the ruled was the *devşirme* (recruitment) system. This was a periodic levy of the male children of Christian subjects, which reduced them to the status of slaves and trained them for the service of the state, either in the military or in the civilian bureaucracy. This system, although not unknown in some earlier Islamic states, was practiced to such an extent that, in time, freeborn Muslims were almost entirely excluded from the administration and the army. As Gibb and Bowen observe,

> whereas in its earlier days the administration of the growing Empire had been conducted by free Muslims, now these were almost without exception replaced by the Sultan's slaves on an ever larger scale, until nearly every post, in what has been described as the "Ruling Institution," of the Empire, was filled either by a Christian conscript or by a slave otherwise acquired. . . . The Ottoman Empire was a Moslem state in which it was paradoxical that any institution should be reserved for the infidel born.[8]

Another difference between Western European feudalism and the Ottoman state system concerns the position of the religious class. In contrast to the autonomous position of the Catholic Church vis-à-vis the state in Western Europe, the religious class in the Ottoman Empire was a state-service class like the fief holders. This class, comprising the muftis (jurists who interpret Muslim law), qadis (judges), and *müderris* (religious scholars), was all servants of the state appointed by the central government. Therefore, they did not constitute a hierarchy independent of government and played almost no role in limiting the absolute powers of the sultans.

Finally, there were no equivalents in the Ottoman Empire of the self-governing cities and powerful merchant guilds of Western European feudalism. Although the *âhi* organizations (artisan guilds) played an important role in the first two centuries of the empire, they gradually lost their influence and were put under strict government controls. As Halil İnalcık points out, "the independent and powerful position of the guilds in the thirteenth and fourteenth centuries weakened under the centralist system of government of the Ottomans."[9] Mardin agrees, saying that "the change in trade routes caused many of these to shift to internal commerce and to reduce drastically the scale of their undertaking. With time, they almost became indistinguishable from the artisan craftsmen class, the *esnaf*."[10]

Thus, with no hereditary aristocracy comparable to that of Western Europe, no independent church hierarchy, no strong and influential merchant class, no self-governing cities, and a ruling institution almost entirely staffed with persons of slave status, the Ottoman Empire represented a close approximation of Oriental despotism. This dichotomy led to a class division very different from that of the West: "that of *askerî* on the one hand and of their opponents on the other. . . . The saliency of these strata replaced the European saliency of strata connected with the production and distribution of goods and services."[11] In this sense, the cleavage between the center and the periphery was one between the political ins and outs. The ins were "the incumbents of the Ottoman institutions. The outs were people who were excluded from the state."[12]

The Rise of Local Notables and the Nineteenth-Century Reforms

Certain changes in the Ottoman society in the eighteenth century brought about some important new dimensions to this picture. One was the emergence of a strong peripheral force of *âyans* (local notables) in the provinces as an intermediary group between the rulers and the ruled. The other was the fragmentation of the old consensus at the center as a result of the growing impact of the West. The *âyans* were not government employees, but were elected by the local people presumably to represent their interests vis-à-vis governmental authorities, especially in matters of tax assessment. However, their elections were recognized by a *ferman* (rescript) by the central government. Their status seems to have derived from ownership of land, legally or illegally converted from fiefs, and wealth obtained through *iltizam* (tax farming) and leasing practices. This was a radical change in the Ottoman land tenure system since, as Gibb and Bowen point out, "in the original scheme of landholding there would appear to have been no place for such persons."[13]

Significantly for the present study, in this modified center-periphery dichotomy, the "silent majority" (the peasants) generally sided with the *âyans*, rather than with the representatives of the central government. While in some cases the *âyans* were no less exploitative in their dealings with the peasantry than the state, "at least they saw it was in their interest to provide those minimum services that kept the system going."[14] "The *âyans* and the peasantry were driven into the same camp, if only because their antagonism to official policy was more enduring than their differences."[15] The alliance between the *âyans* and the peasants continued throughout the Tanzimat (nineteenth-century reform period) against the centrally driven and centralizing reforms. Thus, as İnalcık observes, in contrast to the Balkans where the Christian peasants were ready to rebel to obtain the promises of the Tanzimat, the Anatolian notables were usually able to incite the conservative Muslim peasants against the central government and to take them as allies.[16]

The growing influence of the *âyans* can best be observed in a significant constitutional document called the Sened-i İttifak (Deed of Agreement), which was signed in 1808 between the representatives of the *âyans* and those of the central government. The first of its kind in the Ottoman history and very much against the autocratic tradition of the empire, this agreement provided for mutual support between them and recognized the status of the *âyans*. "Thus, at the dawn of the nineteenth century," observes Bernard Lewis, "the Sultan was brought to Runnymede, to sign a charter that gave formal recognition to feudal rights and autonomies in the Ottoman Empire."[17]

The original center-periphery dichotomy was also modified and complicated by another development; namely, the introduction of European-inspired modernizing reforms. The adoption of, first, Western military technology and, then, Western laws and administrative practices was strongly opposed by the ulema (the old religious class) and the Janissaries (the old military class). This opposition was motivated not only by religious grounds, but also by the fear that such reforms would undermine the bases of their power and status in the society. In contrast to the center-periphery cleavage described above, this one was located at the very center and had an intraelite character. However, it also changed the alliances within the periphery. As the modernizing bureaucratic center became more and more secularized, Islam was increasingly identified with the peripheral culture. Modernization of educational institutions and mass media, as argued by Mardin,

> perpetuated the pre-modern, cultural cleavage between the center and the periphery. . . . A clinging to Islam, to its cultural patrimony, was the province's response to the center's inability to integrate it into the new cultural framework. The provinces thus became centers of "reaction." Most significant, however, was the fear that the provincial world as a whole, including both upper and lower classes, was now increasingly united by an Islamic opposition to secularism. . . . In this new-found unity, the periphery was challenged by a new and intellectually more uncompromising type of bureaucrat.[18]

The new configurations at the center and the periphery have had long-lasting effects on the later political developments in Turkey. First, peripheral and religious oppositions to the centralizing and secularizing bureaucracy were often merged into one, rendering it difficult for even the experienced political analysts to distinguish the elements of the two from each other. Although the church-state cleavage is also found in most Western societies, as analyzed in Chapter 1, it displayed a fundamentally different character in the Ottoman Empire and contemporary Turkey. While in Western societies, secularization was carried out chiefly by the rising bourgeoisie, in the Ottoman Empire it was the central military and bureaucratic elites that were the main force behind secularization against a religious and conservative periphery. Therefore, in this case, the center-periphery and the church-state cleavages were inextricably linked to each other. Second, the merger of the two cleavages gave the peripheral-Islamic opposition a much stronger command of popular loyalties than the centralizing/secularizing official elites can ever hope to enjoy. This provided an almost irresistible temptation for the dissident factions of the central elite to appeal to the sentiments of the peripheral-Islamic opposition in their quest for political power, as shown below.

Another cleavage, which appeared in the second half of the nineteenth century, pitted the constitutionalists (called the Young Ottomans) against the supporters of the autocratic reforms. This was also an intraelite conflict since both sides came from the ranks of the Westernized official elite. As Erik Zürcher observes, the Young Ottomans criticized the Tanzimat reforms "as superficial imitations of Europe without regard for traditional Ottoman and Islamic values, and as subservient to European interests. They also saw the regime of the *Tanzimat* as a one-sided bureaucratic despotism, which had destroyed the older system of checks and balances that had supposedly existed in the empire when the *ulema* still had a more independent and powerful position."[19] Thus, they attempted to combine liberal and Islamic values, and legitimized a constitutional monarchy by references to the old Islamic concepts of *şûra* (consultation) and *baya* (the oath of allegiance to a new ruler). As Zürcher further argues, "the Young Ottomans were a small group within the ruling elite, whose organized activities spanned no more than five years. They were never tightly organized and the ideas of the individual members of the group differed widely. Nevertheless, their influence in Turkey and beyond has been disproportionate. They certainly influenced . . . the introduction of the Ottoman constitution in 1876."[20]

The First and Second Constitutional Periods

The Young Ottomans' advocacy of parliamentarism caused a dilemma for them. Even though they were a part of the central elite and ardent supporters of modernization, they soon realized that when a parliament was convened, it "did not increase the power of the modernizing officials vis-à-vis the Sultan, but . . . rather increased the power of notables against state officials. Thus, the attempt to use parliamentary representation as a means of weakening the power of the Sultan produced the unintended consequence of weakening the State bureaucracy as a power base."[21] Indeed, when the first Ottoman parliament convened in 1877–1878, it included many such notables since the provincial councils that elected the deputies "consisted mainly of notables, *ulema*, and the communal representatives of the non-Muslims."[22]

The Constitution of 1876 attempted to introduce a division of powers between the sultan and parliament, even though the sultan remained the centerpiece of the constitutional system. Nevertheless, even this limited experience in constitutional government proved too much for Abdühamid II, the sultan who prorogued the Chamber of Deputies indefinitely in 1878 and returned to absolute rule for thirty years.[23]

Abdühamid's autocratic policies increasingly alienated the modernizing bureaucratic and military elites who saw a return to constitutionalism as the most effective remedy to the plight of the empire. Lewis accurately describes the intraelite character of this opposition:

> the government of Turkey was still the accepted and recognized prerogative of an *élite* of professionals, who retained all the rights and duties of politics, including that of opposition. It was, therefore, among the servants of the state that the pioneers of revolutionary change emerged; it was in the schools—those nurseries of the civil and military *élite*, so carefully tended by the Sultan himself—that the seeds of revolution were sown.[24]

Eventually, the rebellion of some military units in 1908 forced Abdühamid to restore the constitution.

The November–December 1908 elections for the Chamber of Deputies gave the Young Turks, organized under the party name of the Committee of Union and Progress (CUP), a clear majority in the chamber. The policies of the CUP can be described as centralist, nationalist, authoritarian, statist, and secularist.[25] It essentially represented the central official elite. Even though the party also attracted the support of some local notables and nominated them for parliament in certain provinces, it harbored a deep suspicion of them because of their demands for decentralization. According to Sina Akşin, the real recruitment criteria for the party were Turkishness, youth, education, and belonging to the official class.[26]

The CUP's policies produced two types of opposition. The first was the liberal opposition that favored parliamentary democracy, Ottomanism (i.e., the policy of creating a common bond among different ethnic and religious groups on the basis of loyalty to a common state and the Ottoman throne), secularism, and decentralization. Especially because of its emphasis on decentralization, it was joined by non-Turkish communities (Arabs, Albanians, Greeks, and Armenians). This tendency was also represented by such parties as the Ahrar (Liberal Party), and Mutedil Hürriyetperveran (Moderate Liberals). However, these parties' advocacy of decentralization did not turn them into parties of the periphery. Indeed, they were unable to establish strong roots in the provinces and, thus, remained essentially an intraelite opposition.

The second type was the Islamist opposition that opposed the secularist aspects of the CUP's policies. It found its most radical political expression in the İttihad-ı Muhammedî Fırkası (Muhammedan Union Party). The short-lived unsuccessful revolt of 12–13 April 1909 (known as the "31 March Incident") was carried out by cooperation between the liberal and Islamic oppositions. As Zürcher observes, "most probably the liberal opposition was the original instigator of the revolt. Overestimating its own strength, it thought it could use the religious groups, but soon after the start of the revolt it became clear that it was in no position to exert control."[27]

In 1911, almost all opposition groups were merged under the name of the Hürriyet ve İtilâf (Liberal Union), which brought together Westernized liberals, Islamic traditionalists, and non-Turkish communities. According to Zürcher, "this was a conglomerate of conservatives and liberals with hardly anything in common apart from their hatred for the CUP."[28] Starting in 1913, however, the CUP regime was transformed into an essentially de facto one-party regime that effectively put an end to multiparty competition. This period lasted until 1918, when the CUP regime collapsed with the defeat of the Ottoman Empire in World War I.

The Period of National Liberation, 1920–1923

With the occupation of Istanbul by the Allied military forces and the dissolution of the last Ottoman Chamber of Deputies, an Assembly "with extraordinary powers" (practically meaning a "Constituent Assembly") was convened in Ankara on 23 April 1920. This was in theory a partyless assembly; however, there soon developed a cleavage between the radical revolutionaries under the leadership of Mustafa Kemal Atatürk, the First Group, and the more conservative and liberal deputies, the Second Group. According to Frederick Frey's findings, there were 197 deputies in the First Group, 118 in the Second Group, and 122 who had no ties with either group and did not play an active role in the Assembly.[29] Frey also found differences between the occupational compositions of the two groups. On one hand, the Second Group had higher percentages of lawyers (24 percent as opposed to 9 percent) and merchants (14 percent as opposed to 10 percent). The First Group, on the other hand, had a higher percentage of deputies belonging to "official" occupations; namely, military, bureaucracy, and education (46 percent as opposed to 37 percent). The percentage of deputies belonging to religious occupations was about the same in the two groups (13 percent and 15 percent).[30]

Ideologically, the First Group was composed of radical reformers, even though Atatürk did not reveal his intention of abolishing the monarchy and declaring a republic until after the final victory over the invading Greek army. The Second Group represented a conservative/liberal outlook and was in favor of maintaining a constitutional monarchy.[31] In a way, this was a reincarnation of the cleavage between the CUP and the liberal/conservative opposition during the Second Constitutional Period, a pattern soon to be repeated after the proclamation of the republic in 1923.

The Cleavage Within the Revolutionary Cadres and the Emergence of a Single-Party System

The 1923 elections for the second term of the Grand National Assembly of Turkey (henceforth to be referred to as the "Assembly") took place under the strict control of the People's Party (HF) founded by Atatürk. Consequently, no member of the Second Group was reelected and the Assembly was practically a single-party assembly with all members belonging to the HF.[32] However, a new cleavage soon developed within the ranks of the HF that was reminiscent of the earlier ones. In November 1924, a group of the HF deputies, including some of the closest comrades-in-arms of Atatürk during the War of National Liberation (e.g., Kazım Karabekir, Rauf Orbay, Ali Fuat Cebesoy, Refet Bele, and Adnan Adıvar), resigned from the party and established an opposition party, the Progressive Republican Party (TCF).[33]

Ideologically, the TCF represented a liberal/conservative line and favored a more gradual and evolutionary change. Its party program stated that the TCF's fundamental principles were liberalism and popular sovereignty (democracy). It also stated that the party would be respectful of "religious thoughts and beliefs." It advocated direct (instead of two-stage) election of deputies, decentralization, and the minimization of state functions. In the words of Zürcher, "it was a party in the Western European liberal mould. It stood for secular and nationalist policies, like the majority party, but it clearly opposed its radical, centralist and authoritarian tendencies."[34]

The cleavage between the HF and the TCF can be considered a reemergence of the cleavage between the CUP and the liberal opposition in the Second Constitutional Period, with the HF replacing the CUP. Indeed, it has been shown that many of the middle- or lower-level cadres of the CUP joined the nationalist camp during the War of National Liberation and later the HF.[35] This cleavage, like the earlier ones, was an essentially intraelite conflict. As Lewis observes, "it is . . . very difficult to isolate and identify any clear economic factors or forces in the earlier phases of the Turkish revolutionary struggle. The contenders for power were different groups or factions within the governing *élite*—all of them dependent on the state for a livelihood, and regarding the public service as a natural and proper career for men of their kind."[36]

This proposition is strongly supported by Frey's quantitative data on the background of deputies who belonged to the two parties. Interestingly, the TCF was more strongly dependent on the state elites. Consequently, 76 percent of the TCF parliamentary group had official professions, as opposed to 52 percent of the HF group. The percentage of deputies from a military background was 44 percent in the TCF and 18 percent in the HF. On the other hand, the percentages of deputies belonging to professional or economic occupations were much lower than those of the HF: 16 percent to 21 percent for professional occupations, and 4 percent to 15 percent for economic occupations. Frey concludes from this that "this was an opposition that drew from the very same sources as the Kemalists—intellectuals, bureaucrats, and especially military men. As such, it was possibly the most pernicious development of all in Kemalist eyes, for if successful it threatened to undermine the very foundation of Kemalist strength! For this reason above all the Progressive Republican Party was crushed."[37] Indeed, the TCF was closed down by the government on June 1925, after a short life of only six months, on the fabricated accusation of involvement in the Kurdish revolt in the southeast. A year later, some of its deputies were condemned to death by the extraordinary Court of Independence, again on highly dubious accusations of having been involved in an assassination attempt against Atatürk.[38]

Frey describes this schism within the original revolutionary cadres as a "post independence crisis" that is observed in many newly independent countries. Thus, he argues,

> in this post independence crisis we frequently find arrayed against one another, on one side the charismatic leader and many of his loyal followers . . . and, opposed to them, many of the erstwhile lieutenants of the charismatic leader in the national struggle together with their followers, a group that we can label the "post independence conservatives." . . . More often than not recently, the ardent nationalists seem to win—no doubt partly as a result of their greater unity and discipline, the

carry-over of some of the momentum of the independence struggle, their control over the nationalist organization, and their initial strategic location in the army and government.[39]

These observations accurately describe the Turkish case.

The Single-Party Era

With the closure of the TCF, the adoption of the draconian Takrir-i Sükûn Kanunu (Law on the Maintenance of Order), and the activities of the extraordinary Court of Independence, a single-party system was consolidated, although the de facto monopoly of the single party, now named the Republican People's Party (CHP), was never officially and formally declared. Thus, the postindependence crisis ended with the definite victory of the group, which Frey calls the "ardent nationalists."[40] This change was also reflected in the changing occupational composition of the Grand National Assembly since the weight of the official elites increased sharply. Thus, as opposed to 43 percent of deputies belonging to official occupations in the first Assembly (1920–1923), this figure rose to 54 percent in the 1923 and 1927 Assemblies, and was stabilized at around 45–48 percent in the following legislative terms. In contrast, the percentage of deputies from agricultural and commercial occupations fell from 19 percent in 1920 to 14 percent in 1923. More tellingly, the percentage of deputies with a religious occupation fell from 17 percent in 1920 to 7 percent in 1923, 4 percent in 1927, and about 1 percent in the Assemblies that followed.[41] Thus, with the consolidation process, the more pluralist and representative composition of the First Assembly gave way to the increasing domination of the official elites.

It should not be concluded from this, however, that the social base of the CHP consisted solely of the central military-bureaucratic elite. Like the CUP before it, the CHP was able to attract a number of local notables into its ranks. This was facilitated by the years of close collaboration during the War of National Liberation and effective clientelistic relations. Indeed, many observers describe the CHP as an alliance between the central official elites and the local notables.[42] However, in this alliance the official elites clearly had the upper hand. Thus, according to Frey's analysis, during the single-party period, the Grand National Assembly also included a sizable number of locally based deputies. In general, they were less educated, more rural in origin, and more conservative than deputies from official occupations, but they had considerable influence in their localities. In Frey's words, "in power terms, the elite controlled the major formal institutions of the society, namely the army, the bureaucracy, the educational system. . . . The local leaders controlled the individual villages, towns, and small regions in most aspects of behavior not determined by formally authoritative institutions or by ingrained tradition."[43]

Throughout the single-party years, the CHP maintained the character of an elitist cadre party and never attempted an effective political mobilization of the people.[44] The local organizations of the party generally consisted of local professionals, educators, and notables. The CHP leadership made no notable effort to broaden the party's popular base and to enlist the support of the large peasant masses; instead, it concentrated its attention on the small Westernized elite. As Frey succinctly states,

> the essence of the Atatürk Revolution is that it concentrated on the extension and consolidation of this beachhead to make it secure beyond all possible challenge. . . . It was not . . . a revolution "from the bottom up"—an attempt to remold the society by starting with the peasant masses. Such an attempt was not in keeping with the movement's history nor with the attitudes of its leaders. Moreover, the task was simply too immense for such an approach. As in most emerging nations, a smaller handle was necessary, a lever more easily grasped.[45]

Thus, the Turkish single party fits Samuel P. Huntington's "exclusionary single-party" category. The origins of single-party systems, he argues, lie in a sharp social bifurcation:

> The party is the means by which the leaders of one social force dominate the other social force. . . . With respect to the cleavage and the subordinate social force, the political leaders can follow

one or a combination of two policies. On the one hand, they can accept the bifurcation of the society and use the party as a means of mobilizing support from their constituency while at the same time suppressing or restricting political activity by the subordinate social force. In effect, the party maintains its monopoly over political participation by limiting the scope of political participation. . . . Alternatively, the party leadership can attempt to eradicate the bifurcation of society . . . through liquidation of the subordinate social force or by expanding its constituency to correspond to society by the assimilation of the subordinate social force.

Huntington terms the first type as "exclusionary," and the second type as "revolutionary," single-party systems.[46]

In the Turkish case, the bifurcation was between the Westernized official elites and their allies and the mass of traditional peasantry; the consolidation of the CHP regime marked the domination of the former over the latter. The CHP was conceived not as a mass-mobilizing party, but as an instrument for "enlightening and guiding" the nation. Atatürk explained in a 1925 speech, for example, that the "CHP is not a party engaged in common street politics as in other countries. . . . People's Party has the duty of enlightening and guiding the entire nation. Those who attribute common politicking to our Party are ungrateful. The country needs a solidary unity. To break up the nation by way of ordinary politics is treason."[47]

Expectedly, the scope of political participation was extremely narrow during the single-party years. Even though parliamentary elections were held every four years, the electoral system was an indirect (two-stage) one and all nominees belonged to the CHP. Furthermore, with the 1927 change in the party constitution, nominations came to be made by a triumvirate composed of Atatürk (party chairman and the president of the republic), İsmet İnönü (deputy party chairman and the prime minister), and the secretary-general of the party. Beginning with the 1931 elections, the CHP left a small number of seats open for independents by nominating fewer party candidates than the number of deputies to be elected in each constituency. Societal pluralism was also limited. After the suppression of the TCF in 1925, no political opposition was allowed. The authoritarian character of the regime became more marked from 1931 onward and certain leading nonpolitical voluntary associations were forced to dissolve themselves.[48]

Thus, the single-party era in Turkey can be characterized as the imposed domination of the center and the exclusion and subordination of the periphery. In this sense, it further deepened and intensified the age-old cleavage in Turkish society. The rigid nationalist and secularist policies of the CHP sowed the seeds of deeper ethnic and religious cleavages that came to the surface after the transition to a multiparty system, which I analyze in the following chapter.

Notes

1. Şerif Mardin, "Center-Periphery Relations: A Key to Turkish Politics?" *Dædalus* 2, no. 1 (1973): 169–190. The article was reprinted in Engin D. Akarlı with Gabriel Ben-Dor, eds., *Political Participation in Turkey: Historical Background and Present Problems* (Istanbul: Boğaziçi University, 1975), pp. 7–32. My references are to the reprint. The center-periphery paradigm has been adopted by a number of Turkish scholars: Ergun Özbudun, *Social Change and Political Participation in Turkey* (Princeton: Princeton University Press, 1976), chap. 2; Metin Heper, *The State Tradition in Turkey* (Walkington, UK: Eothen Press, 1985); Metin Heper, "Center and Periphery in the Ottoman Empire with Special Reference to the Nineteenth Century," *International Political Science Review* 1, no. 1 (1980): 81–105; Ersin Kalaycıoğlu, *Turkish Dynamics: Bridge Across Troubled Lands* (New York: Palgrave Macmillan, 2005), pp. 50–53; İlkay Sunar and Sabri Sayarı, "Democracy in Turkey: Problems and Prospects," in Guillermo O'Donnell, Philippe C. Schmitter, and Lawrence Whitehead, eds., *Transitions from Authoritarian-Rule: Southern Europe* (Baltimore: Johns Hopkins University Press, 1986), pp. 166–174. Other authors have referred to the same cleavage under different labels. For example, Emre Kongar argues that the fundamental cleavage in Turkish politics is between the "statist-elitist" and the "traditionalist-liberal" fronts: Emre Kongar, *Türkiye'nin Toplumsal Yapısı*, vol. 1 (Istanbul: Remzi Kitabevi, 1985), pp. 143–144. İdris Küçükömer, a leading economic historian, refers to the same cleavage as one between the "Islamist-Easternist" and "Westernist-Secular" fronts. However, in contrast to the

generally prevailing view, he describes the former as leftist and the latter as rightist. İdris Küçükömer, *Düzenin Yabancılaşması: Batılaşma* (Istanbul: Ant Yayınları, n.d.), p. 82.

2. Mardin, "Center-Periphery Relations," p. 9.

3. Ibid., pp. 12–13.

4. Halil İnalcık, "The Nature of Traditional Society: Turkey," in Robert E. Ward and Dankwart A. Rustow, eds., *Political Modernization in Japan and Turkey* (Princeton: Princeton University Press, 1964), p. 44.

5. For such analyses, see Mardin, "Center-Periphery Relations," pp. 9–15; see also Şerif Mardin, "Historical Determinants of Social Stratification: Social Class and Class Consciousness in Turkey," *A.Ü. Siyasal Bilgiler Fakültesi Dergisi* 22 (1967): 111–142; Özbudun, *Social Change and Political Participation in Turkey*, pp. 21–27; see also Ergun Özbudun, "The Ottoman Legacy and the Middle East State Tradition," in L. Carl Brown, ed., *Imperial Legacy: The Ottoman Imprint on the Balkans and the Middle East* (New York: Columbia University Press, 1996), pp. 133–157; İnalcık, "Nature of Traditional Society," pp. 42–63; H. A. R. Gibb and Harold Bowen, *Islamic Society and the West*, vol. 1 (London: Oxford University Press, 1950), pp. 43–52; Perry Anderson, *Lineages of the Absolutist State* (London: Verso, 1979), pp. 360–431, 482–549.

6. Quoted in Anderson, *Lineages of the Absolutist State,* p. 397.

7. Gibb and Bowen, *Islamic Society and the West,* p. 52.

8. Ibid., pp. 43–45.

9. Halil İnalcık, "The Ottoman Economic Mind and Aspects of the Ottoman Economy," in M. A. Cook, ed., *Studies in the Economic History of the Middle East from the Rise of Islam to the Present Day* (London: Oxford University Press, 1970), p. 216.

10. Mardin, "Historical Determinants of Social Stratification," p. 123.

11. Ibid., p. 127.

12. Engin Deniz Akarlı, "The State as a Socio-cultural Phenomenon and Political Participation in Turkey," in Engin D. Akarlı with Gabriel Ben-Dor, eds., *Political Participation in Turkey: Historical Background and Present Problems* (Istanbul: Boğaziçi University, 1975), p. 139.

13. Gibb and Bowen, *Islamic Society and the West*, pp. 193–199, 253–257; Bernard Lewis, *The Emergence of Modern Turkey* (London: Oxford University Press, 1966), pp. 446–447; İnalcık, "Nature of Traditional Society," pp. 47–48; İlkay Sunar, *State, Society and Democracy in Turkey* (Istanbul: Bahçeşehir University, n.d.), p. 37. On the rise of the class of notables in the Arab provinces of the Ottoman Empire, see Albert Hourani, "Ottoman Reform and the Politics of Notables," in

William R. Polk and Richard L. Chambers, eds., *Beginnings of Modernization in the Middle East: The Nineteenth Century* (Chicago: University of Chicago Press, 1968), pp. 41–68.

14. Mardin, "Center-Periphery Relations," p. 14.

15. Mardin, "Historical Determinants of Social Stratification," pp. 131–132.

16. İnalcık, "Nature of Traditional Society," pp. 59–61.

17. Lewis, *Emergence of Modern Turkey,* p. 448.

18. Mardin, "Center-Periphery Relations," p. 19.

19. Erik J. Zürcher, *Turkey: A Modern History* (London: I. B. Tauris, 1994), pp. 71–72. For a comprehensive analysis of the ideas of the Young Ottomans, see Şerif Mardin, *The Genesis of Young Ottoman Thought: A Study in the Modernization of Turkish Political Ideas* (Princeton: Princeton University Press, 1962).

20. Zürcher, *Turkey,* pp. 73–74.

21. Akarlı, "The State as a Socio-cultural Phenomenon," p. 143.

22. Kemal H. Karpat, "The Transformation of the Ottoman State, 1789–1908," *International Journal of Middle East Studies* 3, no. 3 (1972): 263, 268–270. Robert Devereux describes the first Ottoman parliament as follows: "The deputies represented every social class and economic stratum of the Empire, virtually every religious community and every ethnic and linguistic group. The Chamber was the mosaic of the Empire in miniature; and from that point of view . . . the Chamber was truly a representative body in the fullest sense of that term." Robert Devereux, *The First Ottoman Constitutional Period: A Study of the Midhat Constitution and Parliament* (Baltimore: Johns Hopkins University Press, 1963), pp. 147–148.

23. Ergun Özbudun, *The Constitutional System of Turkey: 1876 to the Present* (New York: Palgrave Macmillan, 2011), pp. 3–4.

24. Lewis, *Emergence of Modern Turkey,* pp. 194–195, 206.

25. On the CUP, see ibid., pp. 213–219; Zürcher, *Turkey,* pp. 90–94; Feroz Ahmad, *The Young Turks: The Committee of Union and Progress in Turkish Politics, 1908–14* (Oxford: Clarendon Press, 1969); Şükrü Hanioğlu, *Preparation for a Revolution: The Young Turks, 1902–1908* (New York: Oxford University Press, 2000); Sina Akşin, *Jön Türkler ve İttihat ve Terakki* (Istanbul: Gerçek Yayınevi, 1980); Tarık Zafer Tunaya, *Türkiye'de Siyasal Partiler,* vol. 1: *İkinci Meşrutiyet Dönemi, 1908–1918* (Istanbul: Hürriyet Vakfı Yayınları, 1984).

26. Akşin, "İttihat ve Terakki Üzerine," *AÜ Siyasal Bilgiler Fakültesi Dergisi* 26, no. 2 (1971): 169–172; see also Karpat, "Transformation of the Ottoman State," pp. 280–281.

27. Zürcher, *Turkey*, pp. 103–104; for the liberal and Islamist oppositions in this era, see pp. 104–108; Tunaya, *Türkiye'de Siyasal Partiler*, pp. 131–363; Akşin, *Jön Türkler ve İttihat ve Terakki*, pp. 98–102, 193–194.

28. Zürcher, *Turkey*, p. 107; Tunaya, *Türkiye'de Siyasal Partiler*, pp. 263–312; Akşin concurs, saying that the Liberal Union was composed of extremely heterogeneous groups united only in the goal of overthrowing the CUP government. It included "socialists, capitalists, feudalminded, various nationalities, Islamists, secularists, Westernists." Akşin, *Jön Türkler ve İttihat ve Terakki*, p. 193.

29. Frederick W. Frey, *The Turkish Political Elite* (Cambridge: MIT Press, 1965), p. 307.

30. Ibid., pp. 310–312.

31. About the composition of and the political controversies in the First National Assembly (1920–1923), see İhsan Güneş, *Birinci Türkiye Büyük Millet Meclisinin Düşünsel Yapısı, 1920–1921* (Eskisehir, Turkey: Anadolu Üniversitesi Yayını, 1985); Ergun Özbudun, *1921 Anayasası* (Ankara: Atatürk Araştırma Merkezi, 1992); Mahmut Goloğlu, *Üçüncü Meşrutiyet, 1920* (Ankara: Başnur Matbaası, 1971); Ömür Sezgin, *Türk Kurtuluş Savaşı ve Siyasal Rejim Sorunu* (Ankara: Birey ve Toplum Yayıncılık, 1984); Elaine Diana Smith, *Turkey: Origins of the Kemalist Movement and Government of the Grand National Assembly* (Washington, DC: Judd & Detweiler, 1959); Rıdvan Akın, *TBMM Devleti* (Istanbul: İletişim, 2001); Fahri Çoker, *Türk Parlâmento Tarihi, Millî Mücadele ve TBMM Birinci Dönem* (Ankara: Türkiye Büyük Millet Meclisi, 1995); Ahmet Demirel, *Birinci Mecliste Muhalefet* (Istanbul: İletişim, 2009); Cemil Koçak, *Birinci Meclis* (Istanbul: Sabancı Üniversitesi, 1998); Taha Akyol, *Atatürk'ün İhtilal Hukuku* (Istanbul: Doğan Kitap, 2012); Michael M. Finefrock, "The Second Group in the First Grand National Assembly," *Journal of South Asia and Middle Eastern Studies*, 3, no. 1 (1979): 3–17.

32. For the interesting story of a single independent deputy (Dulkadirbeyoğlu Zeki Bey) who managed to get elected, see Akyol, *Atatürk'ün İhtilal Hukuku*, pp. 268–271; for a general analysis of this controlled election, see pp. 253–274.

33. On the TCF, see Erik Jan Zürcher, *Political Opposition in the Early Turkish Republic: The Progressive Republican Party, 1924–1925* (Leiden: E. J. Brill, 1991); Nevin Yurtsever Ateş, *Türkiye Cumhuriyetinin Kuruluşu ve Terakkiperver Cumhuriyet Fırkası* (Istanbul: Sarmal Yayınevi, 1994); Ali Fuat Cebesoy, *Siyasi Hâtıralar*, vol. 2 (Istanbul: Doğan Kardeş Yayınları, 1960); Mete Tunçay, *Türkiye Cumhuriyetinde*

Tek-Parti Sisteminin Kurulması, 1923–1931 (Ankara: Yurt Yayınları, 1981), pp. 99–126; Frey, *Turkish Political Elite,* pp. 323–335.

34. Zürcher, *Turkey,* p. 176. For the program of the TCF, see Tunçay, *Türkiye Cumhuriyetinde Tek-Parti Yönetiminin Kurulması,* pp. 370–376.

35. Erik J. Zürcher, *The Unionist Factor: The Role of the Committee of Union and Progress in the Turkish National Movement* (Leiden: E. J. Brill, 1984).

36. Lewis, *Emergence of Modern Turkey,* pp. 463–485.

37. Frey, *Turkish Political Elite,* p. 334.

38. For these events, Zürcher, *Turkey,* pp. 176–182; Akyol, *Atatürk'ün İhtilal Hukuku,* pp. 443–506.

39. Frey, *Turkish Political Elite,* pp. 410–411.

40. For a detailed account of the establishment and consolidation of the single-party regime, see Tunçay, *Türkiye Cumhuriyetinde Tek-Parti Yönetiminin Kurulması.*

41. Frey, *Turkish Political Elite,* pp. 180–184, esp. table 7.5.

42. For example, Dankwart A. Rustow, "The Military: Turkey," in Robert E. Ward and Dankwart A. Rustow, eds., *Political Modernization in Japan and Turkey* (Princeton: Princeton University Press, 1964), p. 388.

43. Frey, *Turkish Political Elite,* pp. 89–98, 133–134; quotation is on p. 134.

44. On the nature of the CHP single-party regime, see Ergun Özbudun, "The Nature of the Kemalist Political Regime," in Ali Kazancıgil and Ergun Özbudun, eds., *Atatürk: Founder of a Modern State,* 2nd ed. (London: C. Hurst, 1997), pp. 79–102; Ergun Özbudun, *Otoriter Rejimler, Seçimsel Demokrasiler ve Türkiye* (Istanbul: Bilgi Üniversitesi Yayınları, 2011), chap. 5.

45. Frey, *Turkish Political Elite,* p. 40; see also Dankwart A. Rustow, "Atatürk as Founder of a State," in *Prof. Dr. Yavuz Abadan'a Armağan* (Ankara: Ankara Üniversitesi Siyasal Bilgiler Fakültesi, 1969), p. 569.

46. Samuel P. Huntington, "Social and Institutional Dynamics of One-Party Systems," in Samuel P. Huntington and Clement H. Moore, eds., *Authoritarian Politics in Modern Society: The Dynamics of Established One-Party Systems* (New York: Basic Books, 1970), p. 15.

47. *Atatürk'ün Söylev ve Demeçleri II, 1906–1938* (Ankara: Türk Tarih Kurumu Basımevi, 1959), p. 224. On the solidarist, corporatist, and authoritarian aspects of the Kemalist ideology, see Ergun Özbudun, "Turkey: Plural Society and Monolithic State," in Ahmet T. Kuru and Alfred Stepan, eds., *Democracy, Islam, and Secularism in Turkey* (New York: Columbia University Press, 2012), pp. 70–82; Taha Parla,

Türkiye'de Siyasal Kültürün Resmî Kaynakları, 3 vols. (Istanbul: İletişim, 1991–1992); Taha Parla and Andrew Davison, *Corporatist Ideology in Kemalist Turkey: Progress or Order?* (Syracuse: Syracuse University Press, 2004); Murat Belge, *Militarist Modernleşme: Almanya, Japonya ve Türkiye* (Istanbul: İletişim, 2011), pp. 539–753.

48. Özbudun, *Otoriter Rejimler, Seçimsel Demokrasiler ve Türkiye*, pp. 80–114; Esat Öz, *Otoriterizm ve Siyaset* (Ankara: Yetkin Yayınevi, 1996); Çetin Yetkin, *Türkiye'de Tek-Parti Yönetimi, 1930–1945* (Istanbul: Altın Kitaplar, 1983).

3

The Impact of
Social Cleavages

AFTER THE END OF WORLD WAR II, THE CHP LEADERSHIP
made a historical decision to permit the establishment of opposition parties. The causes of this fundamental change and the
process in which it was realized are beyond the scope of the present study.[1] The transition was formally inaugurated, however, by
the formation of the DP on 7 January 1946. The new party was led
by Celal Bayar, always an important figure within the CHP and
Mustafa Kemal Atatürk's last prime minister. Bayar was joined by
three other longtime CHP deputies, Adnan Menderes, Fuat
Köprülü, and Refik Koraltan. This pattern strongly reminds one of
the split of the TCF from the CHP in 1924–1925. In both cases,
the leading cadres of the opposition parties were former members
of the government party.

In contrast to the TCF experience, however, this fact was a
facilitating condition for the transition. The CHP government perceived the DP leadership not as a counterelite that would threaten
the Kemalist legacy, but as part of the Kemalist elite. Columnist
Falih Rıfkı Atay of the official CHP daily *Ulus* describes how the
opposition party was perceived by the government: "We wish success to Celal Bayar in establishing an opposition party loyal to the
cause of Kemalism and to the traditions of the Turkish Revolution.

Celal Bayar has earned a reputation in our party on account of his virtue, honesty, and idealism. Is it possible not to be happy if a leader of his qualifications forms an opposition party to face us?"[2]

Indeed, the ideological differences between the two parties seemed minimal. When Bayar visited President İsmet İnönü to present his party's program before its formal inauguration, the following conversation took place:

> İNÖNÜ: Is there any provision that "we are respectful of religious beliefs," as was in the case of the Progressives?
>
> BAYAR: No, my general. Only there is a provision saying that secularism is not being irreligious.
>
> İNÖNÜ: No problem. Will you make an issue of the primary education campaign and the Village Institutes?
>
> BAYAR: No.
>
> İNÖNÜ: Are there any differences in foreign policy?
>
> BAYAR: No.
>
> İNÖNÜ: Then, everything is all right.[3]

Feroz Ahmad makes the same observation that "both parties had much in common and few areas of disagreement. . . . They differed about as much as the Republican and Democratic parties in the United States and had more in common than the Labour and Conservative parties in Britain."[4] Indeed, the main battle cry of the DP from 1946 to 1950 was further democratization and, especially, an electoral reform that would permit honest elections. In 1950, the CHP government agreed to this reform, and the free elections of 1950 resulted in a landslide victory for the DP, a good example of Samuel P. Huntington's "stunning elections" concept.[5] The DP won three consecutive parliamentary elections in 1950, 1954, and 1957, with comfortable majorities (55.2 percent, 57.6 percent, and 47.9 percent, respectively). The end of the DP domination came with the military coup of 27 May 1960. From 1946 to 1960, the Turkish party system displayed the characteristics of a typical two-party system, as I analyze in Chapter 4.

What sort of social cleavage did this party system reflect, especially in view of the fact that the top leadership of the DP came from the CHP ranks and belonged to the official state elites? Several arguments have been put forward in this regard. One associates the rise of the DP with the growing influence of the commercial bourgeoisie. Thus, it is argued that the CHP's statism, far from being an antibusiness ideology, actually benefited the commercial and industrial sectors by creating an infrastructure, providing cheap intermediary goods, and training the cadres that later assumed managerial positions in the private sector. Continuing with this line of reasoning,

> up to a point the bureaucracy and the commercial classes were able to get along together, but beyond that point the unity of interests broke down. By the end of World War II during which its wealth had increased by leaps and bounds, the bourgeoisie ceased to depend on the protection of the state—in fact, the protections had turned into fetters. . . . The commercial classes were convinced that their security would only be assured by the replacement of the bureaucrats.[6]

There is little empirical evidence, however, that in the mid-1940s the influence of the emerging commercial bourgeoisie had reached a point to force the CHP leadership to such a decision. In fact, the dependence of the private sector on the state continued for a long time, and continues today to a lesser extent.[7] The significant growth of civil society in general and the private business sector in particular started with the promarket, export-oriented policies of the ANAP government (1983–1991), led by Turgut Özal.

Another explanation connects the rise of the DP with the unsuccessful land reform attempt of the CHP government in 1945 and the consequent breaking up of the old alliance between the official elites and landowning local notables. This view also does not seem convincing. It is true that Adnan Menderes (later one of the four founders of the DP and prime minister from 1950 to 1960, himself a large landowner) was one of the sharpest critics of the land reform bill. As I show below, however, many local notables remained loyal to the CHP throughout the 1950s. The DP's appeal was strongest in western Turkey, where the distribution of landownership was more equitable, and not in the east and the southeast, where it was most concentrated. By the same token, it would be incorrect to describe the DP as essentially based on the peasant masses and the 1950 elections as "ruralizing elections." I also show that, in the 1950 elections, the rural votes were about equally divided between the two parties and it was the DP's stronger appeal in urban areas that gave it a majority.

On the basis of these facts, Hakan Yılmaz argues that, at the time of the regime change, the Turkish bourgeoisie had not reached the level of a "class-for-itself" or evolved into the "hegemonic political" stage. Thus, he continues,

> The Turkish bourgeoisie of the 1940s did not apparently possess the organizational and ideological capacity to take the means of administration from the hands of the bureaucracy. . . . The DP . . . was not the party of the Turkish bourgeoisie. . . . The relationship between the DP and the Turkish bourgeoisie, just as the one between the DP and the peasant masses, was not one of political representation but a complete "delegation of will" from the social support base to the party, and from the party rank and file to the party leadership. The regime that resulted in the 1950s from this peculiar relationship between the DP and its support groups in the society resembled what Guillermo O'Donnell called in the Latin American context "delegative democracy."[8]

Thus, the DP was able to appeal successfully to several different peripheral oppositions. One of these included the traditionalist and religious groups that were alienated because of the CHP's radical secularist policies. This does not mean, however, that the DP was essentially an Islamist conservative party. As Frederick W. Frey appropriately argues, the DP, "though willing to support a mild religious 'revival' (actually, a partial easing of previous restraints rather than a revival), was basically quite modern in its top personnel and quite committed in its own way to a continuation of modernization, even while trying to make political capital out of the religious issue."[9] Another peripheral opposition comprised the peasant masses that had suffered from the exclusionary policies and authoritarian practices of the single-party regime in whose eyes the CHP government was symbolized as the gendarmerie and the tax collector. A third one consisted of the non-Muslim groups that were heavily penalized by the regime's discriminatory policies, especially by the draconian Varlık Vergisi (capital levy) of 1942. The opposition coalition was also joined by liberal intellectuals in favor of a democratic regime and by members of the commercial bourgeoisie that advocated a more liberal, promarket economic policy.

The only common features of these different peripheral oppositions were their exclusion from the centers of power and consequent desire to increase their influence and efficacy within the political system. Thus, Ersin Kalaycıoğlu succinctly states that "the DP emerged as the party of the peasants, the neglected, and the downtrodden, businessmen, merchants, or in a nutshell, of the Periphery, challenging the arbitrary, callous, self-centered style of the party of the Center, the CHP, the public bureaucracy, which the DP was bent upon dislodging . . . from the centers of political power in Turkey."[10] İlkay Sunar and Sabri Sayarı similarly argue that

> the DP leadership forged a wide-ranging coalition among a motley of discontented peripheral groups including the more modern (market-oriented) landed interests found in the Western parts of Turkey, the urban mercantile class, most of the small peasantry, and religious protest groups. A wide clientelist network, fed by distributive policies, a diffuse populist appeal, a conciliatory attitude toward religious demands, and a relative liberalization of the economy bound this variety of peripheral groups loosely to the DP.[11]

Since no survey data on voting behavior are available for the 1950s, certain insights can be obtained through ecological voting analysis. Started by Frey[12] and continued by me,[13] this analysis involves looking for correlations between the percentage of the popular vote in each province obtained by each party and a number of socioeconomic indicators such as urbanization, literacy, income per capita, and proportion of the workforce in agriculture. Thus, in the three national elections in the 1950s (those of 1950, 1954, and 1957), the DP obtained its strongest support in the highly developed Marmara and Aegean regions while the CHP's strongholds were generally the least developed eastern regions (Table 3.1).[14] Similarly, at the provincial level Frey found positive correlations between the DP vote and the indicators of provincial socioeconomic development, and negative correlations between the CHP vote and such indicators.[15] On the basis of these findings, he concludes that

> in the 1950s, the Democratic party rested primarily upon the twin supports of the more developed part of the peasantry and an urban coalition of business and free professional elites, together with many working-class people of various types. Its appeal was to the more modern regions of the country and the more privatistic and enterprising elements therein. The statistical manifestations of these tendencies are the consistent, if moderate (0.1 to 0.3), positive correlations between provincial Democratic Party voting percentages and such indicators as literacy, all-weather roads, radio receivers, national taxes collected, and so forth.[16]

This seems paradoxical at first glance. How can we explain the weakness of the CHP, the torchbearer of modernization in the more modern regions, and its relatively stronger position in the least developed ones? One would have expected the opposite, given the CHP's strong identification with modernization policies. One reason may lie in the continued loyalty to the CHP of certain local notables in the latter areas and their ability to mobilize large numbers of their clients to vote for this party.[17] Second, it was quite natural that disappointment with the single-party regime's authoritarian and exclusionary policies was more keenly felt among the socioeconomically more modern sectors of the population. As Joseph La Palombara and Myron Weiner observe, in many countries the emergence of political parties is associated with a "participation crisis"; namely, the desire of excluded social groups to become participants in politics.[18]

Table 3.1   Votes for Major Parties by Region, 1950, 1954, and 1957 (percentages)

	1950		1954		1957	
Region	DP	CHP	DP	CHP	DP	CHP
Turkey	52.7	39.4	57.6	35.4	47.9	41.1
Marmara	55.3	33.7	62.0	29.4	55.3	36.7
Aegean	57.8	40.2	61.3	36.0	53.7	37.3
Mediterranean	55.0	40.9	55.0	39.0	45.3	47.1
North-Central	53.9	36.2	54.2	31.9	42.9	37.0
South-Central	59.8	37.7	56.4	32.0	45.3	38.9
Black Sea	49.7	41.9	57.3	33.7	45.6	41.0
East-Central	48.4	46.0	50.0	44.8	40.9	50.2
North-East	48.8	43.4	52.4	37.8	42.5	44.2
South-East	44.9	47.7	52.2	32.6	47.0	42.7

Source: Percentages are computed by the author based on the official election results published by the State Institute of Statistics.

Notes: I use the ninefold classification of agricultural regions used by Frederic W. Frey and others. The list of provinces in each region is Marmara: Istanbul, Sakarya, Bursa, Kocaeli, Edirne, Tekirdağ, Kırklareli; Aegean: Aydın, Balıkesir, Burdur, Çanakkale, Denizli, Isparta, İzmir, Manisa, Muğla; Mediterranean: Adana, Antalya, Gaziantep, Hatay, İçel, Maraş; North-Central: Ankara, Bilecik, Bolu, Çankırı, Çorum, Eskişehir, Kırşehir, Kütahya, Nevşehir, Uşak, Yozgat; South-Central: Afyon, Kayseri, Konya, Niğde; Black Sea: Giresun, Gümüşhane, Kastamonu, Ordu, Rize, Samsun, Sinop, Trabzon, Zonguldak; East-Central: Adıyaman, Amasya, Elazığ, Malatya, Sivas, Tokat, Tunceli; North-East: Ağrı, Artvin, Erzincan, Erzurum, Kars; South-East: Bingöl, Bitlis, Diyarbakır, Hakkâri, Muş, Siirt, Urfa, Van.

Frey's findings on the background characteristics of deputies also shed some light on the differences between the two parties. Thus, in the Eighth Assembly (1946–1950), 39 percent of the CHP deputies had official occupations as opposed to only 6 percent of the DP deputies, while 33 percent of the DP group were lawyers compared to 18 percent of the CHP group. In other words, "the Democrats were notably more professional and economic and less official in occupation."[19] Similarly, the DP group had more locally born (i.e., born in the provinces they represented) deputies than the CHP group, 67 percent to 56 percent. One must also note that, with the transition to a multiparty system, "the basic social background characteristics of the People's Party had already shown a strong general movement in the direction of the Democratic Party." A comparison between the CHP groups in the Seventh (1943–1946) and Eighth Assemblies reveals that the former contained a higher percentage of deputies belonging to official occupations: 47 percent to 39 percent. Frey concludes that

> despite a major adjustment within the R.P.P. [CHP] in the Eighth Assembly, the Democratic Party still clearly differs from it and is even further down the road along which the People's Party was traveling. . . . Much of the political history of the era is wrapped up in the decline of the officials and the rise of the professional and economic contingents in the Grand National Assembly. The "new man in Turkish politics" is the lawyer and the merchant, replacing the soldier and the bureaucrat at the pinnacle of formal power. . . . The deputies have changed from being primarily a national elite group, oriented toward the tutelary development of the country, to being an assembly of local politicians, oriented toward more immediate local and political advantages.[20]

From the Center-Periphery Cleavage to a Functional Cleavage

The 27 May 1960 military intervention, which ousted the ten-year-long DP government, dissolved the parliament, and established a transitional military ruling committee (National Unity Committee), can be characterized as the revenge of the official elites and their representative in the political arena, the CHP, over the DP. At first glance, this interruption in the democratic process seems to have had important consequences for the party system. The forced dissolution of the DP, the competition of three successor parties (the Justice Party, AP; New Turkey Party, YTP; and preexisting Republican Peasant Nation Party, CKMP) for the former DP votes, and the introduction of a proportional representation system produced a four-party structure in the 1961 Assembly, as I analyze in Chapter 4. However, a closer look at the results of the 1961 elections does not reveal a change in the center-periphery cleavage.

The party of the center, the CHP, won 36.7 percent of the vote in the National Assembly elections and 36.1 percent in the Senate elections, a considerable drop from 41.1 percent in the 1957 elections. The total vote of the three parties that can be considered peripheral oppositions was 62.5 percent in the National Assembly elections: AP, 34.8 percent; YTP, 13.7 percent; and CKMP, 14.0 percent. Clearly, the superiority of the peripheral parties continued and even increased.

This pattern also held in the 1965 elections. The AP, which by that time had established itself as the true heir to the DP, won an absolute majority (53.3 percent) of the National Assembly seats with 52.9 percent of the vote while the CHP further declined to 28.7 percent of the vote. On the other hand, two new minor ideological parties gained representation in the Assembly: the avowedly Marxist TİP (with 3 percent of the vote) and the radical nationalistic Nationalist Action Party (MHP, with 2.2 percent of the vote). Thus, class and ideological cleavages were added to the still-dominant center-periphery cleavage.

The AP represented the same social base of support as the DP and followed essentially the same kind of policies. In the words of Sunar and Sayarı, the AP

> was electorally successful in the 1960s by relying for its support on the business community, agrarian interests, the small peasantry, and urban marginals. In terms not only of its clientelist incorporation of diverse groups, but also of its economic liberalism, its conciliatory and concessionary attitude toward religion, and populist sentimentality, the JP [AP] essentially followed in the footsteps of the DP.[21]

The CHP, on the other hand, faced a dilemma in the face of its declining electoral support in the 1960s. The party's timid opening to the left in the 1965 elections under the "left-of-center" motto resulted in another electoral defeat with a much lower percentage (28.7 percent) of the vote. Furthermore, this shift to the left led to a split within the party. Following the eventful Fourth Extraordinary Congress of the party on 28 April 1967, a group of forty-seven deputies and senators under the leadership of Turhan

Feyzioğlu resigned from the party. This group, which was attached to the old statist and elitist views of the party and uneasy about the move to the left, formed the Reliance Party (GP), which won 6.6 percent of the vote in the 1965 elections.

After the split of the GP and under the energetic leadership of the new secretary-general Bülent Ecevit, the CHP started to follow a more resolute left-of-center policy.[22] The 1969 parliamentary elections, however, proved to be another defeat for the party. Its percentage of the national vote fell to 27.4 percent (even below that of its 1965 showing) against the AP's 46.5 percent. On the other hand, the 1969 elections marked the beginning of a significant change in the support base of the CHP. Thus, compared to its 1965 performance, its percentage of votes rose in the more developed regions and fell in the less developed ones, particularly in the southeastern region (Table 3.2). Also, the CHP vote began to show positive, albeit moderate, correlations with the indicators of provincial socioeconomic development, such as urbanization, literacy, and percentage of male population in the manufacturing

Table 3.2 Votes for Major Parties by Region, 1961, 1965, and 1969 (percentages)

	1961		1965		1969	
Region	AP	CHP	AP	CHP	AP	CHP
Turkey	34.8	36.7	52.9	28.7	46.5	27.4
Marmara	40.6	35.7	57.8	28.0	52.0	30.8
Aegean	55.0	36.4	63.7	27.9	57.5	29.1
Mediterranean	45.7	41.0	56.1	31.9	43.2	29.3
North-Central	27.2	33.5	50.7	26.0	48.0	26.8
South-Central	29.9	33.6	54.6	25.9	50.5	21.0
Black Sea	36.9	35.5	55.8	29.1	46.3	30.7
East-Central	16.2	42.6	41.0	35.4	29.7	27.7
North-East	16.1	39.3	44.7	29.1	46.8	27.4
South-East	10.0	38.1	28.9	28.7	29.9	16.1

Source: Percentages are computed by the author based on the official election results published by the State Institute of Statistics.

Note: I use the ninefold classification of agricultural regions used by Frederic W. Frey and others. See Table 3.1 for a list of the provinces in each region.

industry.[23] This can be explained, on the one hand, by the increasing appeal of the left-of-center policy among the urban working classes and, on the other, by the desertion of the local notables wing of the party after the split of the GP.

This trend continued and markedly strengthened in the 1973 elections, which were held in the aftermath of the semimilitary regime of 1971–1973. The CHP emerged as the strongest party, with 33.3 percent of the national vote (about a 6 percent increase over its percentage of the 1969 vote). On the other hand, the center-right vote was fragmented among three parties: the AP, with 29.8 percent; the Democratic Party (DemP; a group that had split from the AP), with 11.9 percent; and the MNP (a newly established Islamist-oriented party under the leadership of Necmettin Erbakan), with 11.8 percent. Correlations between the percentage of the CHP vote and the indicators of provincial socioeconomic development remained about as strong as in the 1969 elections, but those for the AP grew weaker. One of the most noteworthy characteristics of the 1973 elections was the shift in the large city votes. While the AP lost heavily in the large cities, the CHP substantially increased its urban strength in this period, and a major part of this gain seems to have come from the urban lower classes who responded positively to the party's opening to the left.[24] This trend was confirmed by the local elections of December 1973, in which the CHP won thirty-two of sixty-seven mayoralties in provincial centers, including the four largest cities in Turkey (Istanbul, Ankara, İzmir, and Adana), where such posts had long been held by the AP. The rise of the CHP reached its peak in the 1977 National Assembly elections when it again emerged as the leading party, with 41.4 percent of the vote (its highest percentage in the history of multiparty politics in Turkey thus far) against the AP's 36.9 percent. These changes have been described as a "critical realignment" in the Turkish party system and a shift from the old center-periphery cleavage to a functional left-right (or class) cleavage.[25] Indeed, in this period, the CHP had taken a clear turn to the left under the leadership of Bülent Ecevit, who had replaced the party's historical leader, İnönü, in 1972.

The new CHP not only emphasized such leftist themes as social justice, a more equitable distribution of income, and land reform,[26] but also carefully distanced itself from certain authoritarian elements of the Kemalist ideology. Thus, Ecevit refused to support the semimilitary regime of 1971–1973, marking the break of the alliance between the CHP and the military. Although he never repudiated the Kemalist legacy, Ecevit criticized the reforms of this period as "superstructural reforms" that did not bring any improvements in the standard of living for the masses.[27] Equally important, under his leadership the CHP softened its militant conception of secularism and defined its new position as "secularism respectful of religious beliefs." Clearly, the urban working class, urban professionals, intellectuals, students, and peasants in the more modernized regions of the country responded to these changes positively.

Whether the changes in the party system during this period constitute a secular realignment in the party system, however, is questionable with the benefit of hindsight. V. O. Key Jr. first put forward the concepts of "critical elections" and "secular realignment." He argues,

> Some elections may be "critical" in that they involve far wider movements and more durable shifts than do other elections. . . . Only events with widespread and powerful impact or issues touching deep emotions produce abrupt changes. . . . A secular shift in party attachment may be regarded as a movement of the members of a population category from party to party that extends over several presidential elections and appears to be independent of the peculiar factors influencing the vote at individual elections. . . . How long such a trend should persist to fall within the definition may be left inexact, but a movement that extends over a half century is a more persuasive indication of the existence of the phenomenon in mind than is one that lasts less than a decade.[28]

As mentioned above, many Turkish observers, including me, saw the changes in the Turkish party system in the late 1960s and the 1970s as an example of a critical realignment.[29] Indeed, the Turkish case meets some of the conditions in Key's definition, in that the change involved the movement of a certain population category (i.e., the urban working class) from the AP to the CHP. Also, the rise of Ecevit was surrounded by an aura of trust and charisma that touched on "deep emotions." On the other hand, the ascendancy of the CHP proved to be short-lived, less than even a decade. The 1979 elections for one-third of senators and five vacant seats in the National Assembly were a decisive defeat for the CHP, whose vote fell to 29.1 percent while that of the AP rose to 46.8 percent. Thus, when the 12 September 1980 military coup once again interrupted the democratic process, the balance of power between the two major parties had resumed its position of the mid-1960s. Indeed, in the by-elections of 1979, the AP clearly emerged as the leading party, while the CHP once again fell to a secondary position.

Furthermore, none of the parties that succeeded the CHP in the aftermath of the period of military regime (1980–1983) could even approach its showing in the 1977 elections: in 1983, the Populist Party (HP) at 30.5 percent; in 1987, the Social Democratic Populist Party (SHP) at 24.8 percent and Ecevit's Democratic Left Party (DSP) at 8.5 percent; in 1991, the SHP at 20.8 percent and the DSP at 10.8 percent; in 1995, the CHP (which regained its old name) at 10.7 percent and the DSP at 14.6 percent; in 1999, the CHP at 8.7 percent and the DSP at 22.2 percent. Starting in the early 1990s, the left lost its dominant position in the large cities and its support among the urban poor to the newly rising Islamist RP, which in the 1994 local elections captured the mayoralties of Turkey's two largest cities (Istanbul and Ankara) and those of many other provincial centers. Thus, the trend toward a system of functional cleavages effectively came to an end. After two decades of uncertainty, volatility, and fragmentation, the center-periphery cleavage was restored, although in a somewhat modified form, as I explain below.

A Period of Transition, 1983–2001

The military coup of 12 September 1980 and the following NSC regime (1980–1983) brought about a period of transition in the Turkish party system that was marked by uncertainties, the emergence of new parties, splits or mergers (such as the split of the AP into the ANAP and the DYP, and of the CHP into the HP and SODEP; later on, the merger of the latter two under the name of SHP), and a high degree of volatility. The NSC regime banned all parties that existed on the eve of the intervention in 1980, and did not permit the formation of new ones until three years later. The November 1983 parliamentary elections that marked the transition to a civilian regime were highly controlled, or limited-choice, elections. The NSC permitted only three parties to compete in these elections, two of which can be considered of its own creation. One was the Nationalist Democracy Party (MDP), led by a retired general, Turgut Sunalp, who was close to the NSC regime. The other was the HP, led by a high-level bureaucrat, Necdet Calp, which was designed to play the role of a moderately leftist, loyal opposition party. Two parties, the True Path Party (DYP) and the Social Democratic Party (SODEP), which looked like more credible heirs to the banned major parties (the AP and CHP), were not permitted to contest the elections. The third competing party was the ANAP, led by Özal, which was not truly a creation of the regime even though Özal had served in the NSC cabinet as a deputy prime minister. Furthermore, the NSC even vetoed hundreds of candidates on the lists of the three licensed parties, not to mention having imposed ten- and five-year bans on the political activities of leading cadres and parliamentarians of the preexisting parties. Thus, the 1983 elections were indeed limited-choice elections in the fullest sense.[30]

However, despite all these electoral manipulations, the ANAP, the party least favored by the NSC, emerged as the victor in the 1983 elections with 45.1 percent of the vote and an absolute majority of the Assembly seats. The HP came in second with 30.5 percent, and the NSC's favorite party, the MDP, was third with only 23.3 percent of the vote. The new single-party government of the ANAP was formed under the premiership of Özal. The local elections held a few months later in the spring of 1984, which were contested by all parties, redressed the anomalies of the 1983 elections. Thus, two of the regime-created parties performed badly (the HP with 8.8 percent of the vote and the MDP with 7.1 percent) while the ANAP maintained its position with 41.5 percent. The two successor parties that were not permitted to run in 1983 emerged as the second- and third-largest parties: the SODEP as heir to the CHP, with 23.4 percent, and the DYP as heir to the AP, with 13.3 percent. Shortly thereafter, the HP merged with the SODEP under the name of the SHP and the MDP decided to dissolve itself.

It is not clear what sort of cleavage structure this new party constellation reflected. The HP and the SODEP clearly inherited the former CHP votes and represented a similar political line. However, the ANAP was a new and different phenomenon in Turkish politics. Özal had always described his party as a synthesis of the four preexisting tendencies; namely, conservatism, nationalism, liberalism, and social democracy. In fact, throughout its life, the ANAP was a coalition of conservative, nationalist, and liberal factions. Üstün Ergüder and Richard Hofferbert's study on the results of the 1983 elections shows that the ANAP vote did not correlate significantly with any of the cleavages in the pre-1980 era; namely, center-periphery, left-right, and prosystem-antisystem. They argue that the ANAP was not the reincarnation of any of the preexisting political parties, having found the strongest correlation coefficient (0.5) with the antisystem tendency in the 1960s and the 1970s. This may be due to the fact that a majority of the voters of the two radical (antisystem) parties, the extreme nationalist MHP and the Islamist National Salvation Party (MSP), which were not permitted to run in 1983, voted for the ANAP's candidates. One cannot assume from this, however, that the ANAP was itself an antisystem party. Thus, Ergüder and Hofferbert conclude that the ANAP was essentially a centrist and moderate party that served to integrate formerly antisystem groups into the mainstream politics.[31] Ayşe Ayata similarly argues that, of all the Turkish parties in the 1980s, only the ANAP "is based on new societal cleavages and mobilization of a relatively new ideological concept known as the new right." She observes that whereas some scholars view the ANAP "as an extension of the 1980 coup government," others see it as "the initiator of liberal revolutions, antibureaucratic, pluralist, modern, and able to bring together a coalition including a wide range of ideological groups" and, thus, a "genuine catchall party."[32]

The ANAP's domination did not last long, however. It lost its parliamentary majority in the 1991 elections, and a DYP-SHP coalition government was formed. Throughout the 1990s, both the center-right and the center-left were divided within themselves; the former between the ANAP and the DYP, and the latter between the SHP and the DSP. The main cleavage line in this period can be characterized as a left-right one, with the center-right parties advocating a free-market economic policy and the center-left parties supporting a mixed economy where the state was expected to play a more active role. However, the collapse of the Soviet bloc and the declining appeal of leftist ideologies on a global scale minimized the ideological differences between these two camps. Thus, it is noteworthy that the constitutional amendment of 1999, which explicitly permitted privatization and the possibility of international arbitration in concession contracts involving a foreign party, took place during the coalition government headed by the leftist Ecevit.

The Renewed Saliency of the Center-Periphery Cleavage

The 1990s also witnessed the spectacular rise of the Islamist-oriented RP, a successor to the MSP in the 1970s. The RP was not permitted to run in the 1983 elections, and it obtained only 7.2 percent of the vote in the 1987 elections. But it contested the 1991 elections in alliance with the ultranationalist Nationalist Work Party (MÇP), a successor to the MHP in the 1970s, and the conservative minor party, the Reformist Democracy Party (IDP). The alliance received a total of 16.9 percent of the vote, which enabled it to pass the 10 percent national threshold. However, the spectacular rise of the RP came in the 1994 local elections when it captured the mayoralties of many provincial centers, including those of the two largest cities in Turkey, Istanbul and Ankara. This was followed by its successful performance in the 1995 parliamentary elections when it emerged as the first party, with 21.4 percent of the national vote and 28.7 percent of the Assembly seats. After a brief period of the center-right ANAP-DYP coalition government, the RP was able to form a new coalition government with the DYP under the premiership of the party leader, Erbakan.

The rise to power of the RP deepened the fears of the secularist groups and the military about the gradual introduction of an Islamist regime. These fears led to the so-called postmodern coup of 28 February 1997 whereby pressures from the military forced the Erbakan government to resign and led to the formation of a new coalition government of the ANAP, the DSP, and the Democratic Turkey Party (a group that split from the DYP) with the parliamentary support of the CHP.[33] This was followed by the closure of the RP by the Constitutional Court on 16 January 1998 because of its alleged antisecular activities. Its successor party, the FP, met the same fate on 22 June 2001.

The rise of the Islamist parties and the consequent deepening of the secular-religious cleavage can be characterized as the renewed saliency of the center-periphery cleavage. As indicated above, these two cleavages overlap and reinforce each other significantly in the Turkish case. As the central bureaucratic elites embarked on a program of top-down modernization (read as Westernization), the periphery increasingly identified itself with traditional Islamic values. Parallel to this, the peripheral-religious sectors of the society suffered most under the militantly secularist, authoritarian, and exclusionary policies of the center.

Thus, research on the socioeconomic characteristics of the RP voter base support these observations. Sociologically, the RP was a broad coalition that included a sizable portion of the rural population, the small traders and artisans of Anatolian towns, poor urban migrants, the rising Islamic bourgeoisie, and Islamist professionals and intellectuals. With regard to occupational groups, the RP's support was stronger than its national average among small farmers, manual workers, and small merchants and artisans. Similarly, the RP was overrepresented among lower and lower-middle classes, and underrepresented among middle, upper-middle, and upper classes.[34] The common elements uniting these diverse groups were their attachment to religious-conservative values and their reaction to exclusion from the center of power for a long time. In this sense, it would not be wrong to describe the RP, as well as its predecessors and successors, as the party of the periphery.

With the 2001 closure by the Constitutional Court of the FP (the successor to the RP), the movement split into two parties.

The faction called the *gelenekçiler* (traditionalists) formed the Felicity Party (SP) and remained loyal to the national view ideology of the old party. The faction called the *yenilikçiler* (modernists or innovators), on the other hand, formed the AKP under the leadership of Recep Tayyip Erdoğan, the former mayor of Istanbul. The AKP came to power in the 2002 parliamentary elections with 34.3 percent of the vote and 66 percent of the Assembly seats, while the SP obtained only 2.5 percent of the vote.

The AKP's ideology departed from the national view ideology in some important ways. Hence, the party program expressed much stronger support for a secular system of government, emphasizing such values as democracy, human rights, the rule of law, a free-market economy, and globalization. It presented itself as a "conservative democratic party" instead of a Muslim democratic party.[35] As for its social base, while maintaining the coalitional character of its predecessor, the AKP broadened its appeal to a much larger sector of society. Thus, in the 2002 elections, the AKP seems to have received substantial support from the former voters of the two center-right parties (the ANAP and DYP) and those of the ultranationalist MHP, in addition to more than half of the former Islamist FP voters. Surprisingly, some 10 percent of the former voters of the leftist DSP also indicated their intention to vote for the AKP. Just as the AKP is a coalition of diverse political forces, it is also a coalition in the sociological sense. It is generally described as a "cross-class" coalition encompassing a large part of the rural population, artisans and small traders in the cities and towns, the urban poor, and the rapidly rising Islamic bourgeoisie.[36] Hakan Yavuz sees the "new emerging bourgeoisie rooted in Anatolia" as the driving force of this coalition.[37] Similarly, Ahmet İnsel describes the AKP as "the political representative of the new middle class," comprising provincial artisans and traders, and small- and mid-range entrepreneurs and young business executives, although he adds that the AKP also receives votes from a good portion of the working class.[38] The percentage of votes for the AKP increased to 46.6 percent in the 2007 parliamentary elections, and to 49.8 percent in 2011.

The cleavage structure that emerged in the 1990s and prevails to the present has been described in different ways. One view characterizes it as an essentially left-right cleavage, with the current trend being identified as a swing toward the far right. This argument is based on the strong correlation between party preferences and the voters' self-placement on a left-right scale. Yılmaz Esmer, for example, argues that

> the left-right ideological position is one of the leading indicators—if not the most important one—of voter preferences. . . . The differences are very substantial with the difference between the CHP voters on the far-left and the FP voters on the far-right of the scale being more than 1.7 standard deviations. In the face of these data, it is very hard to confirm the frequently expressed argument that, in the 1990s, the left and right have lost their meanings and have become devoid of their traditional contents.[39]

It can be asked, however, whether this correlation is more spurious than real because it is not clear whether voters prefer certain parties because of their self-placement on a left-right scale, or because they place themselves on such a scale because of their identification with a certain political party for a variety of reasons. Even if the correlation is not spurious, we still have to clarify the meanings of the terms *left* and *right* in Turkish politics, as they are very different from their meanings in Western democracies.

Traditionally in Western democracies, the left-right dimension in politics is associated with party positions on socioeconomic issues. Parties on the left support greater public ownership of the means of production, a stronger governmental rule in economic planning, redistribution of wealth from the rich to the poor, and expansion of public social welfare programs, while parties on the right support the opposite. Interestingly, in the Turkish context these terms are used not in their conventional sense, but refer to a cultural-religious dimension. Thus, the *right* refers to a commitment to religious, conservative, and nationalist values while the *left* is defined primarily in terms of secularism. Furthermore, the positions of Turkish parties on socioeconomic issues do not correspond to the conventional meaning of the left-right cleavage. The center-right, conservative, and Islamist parties have always shown sensitivity to the plight of low-income groups and favored a paternalistic notion of the state. Besides, the collapse of the Soviet bloc and the weakening appeal of leftist ideologies worldwide minimized the differences among parties' positions on socioeconomic issues. Finally, in the 1990s and 2000s, the CHP moved from its moderately leftist positions back to its old secularist and tutelarist legacy, as I discuss in the following chapter. Thus, it is difficult to characterize the CHP as a bona fide leftist or social democratic party, just as it is hard to describe the AKP as a far-right party.

In a real sense, therefore, the center-periphery cleavage rose to prominence again in a somewhat modified and, even deepened, form. The rise of the Islamic-rooted AKP to power created deep fears within the secular camp and its chief representative, the CHP. It has been argued that

> the source of the secular establishment's threat perception is not the policies but the alleged Islamist identity of the JDP [AKP]. Hence, the establishment persistently warns the public of the worrying magnitude of reactionism. . . . The emphasis on the JDP members' Islamist pedigree and conservative life styles rather than on its policy proposals has reinforced the definition of the secular state as a community of devout believers of Kemalism. In fact, this "communitization" of the state during the JDP government has reached unprecedented levels.[40]

Starting in the mid-1980s, a new type of peripheral opposition emerged by the formation of Kurdish nationalist parties. These parties are typical *peripheral opposition parties* in both senses of the term: first, in a geographical sense, since their popular support is concentrated in the southeastern region where Kurds constitute a strong majority; and, second, in a cultural sense, since these parties express the identity-based claims of the long-excluded and discriminated-against Kurdish minority. The first explicitly Kurdish party was the People's Labor Party (HEP), formed by seven Kurdish deputies who were expelled from the SHP. After the closure of the HEP by the Constitutional Court in 1993, it was replaced by the Democracy Party (DEP). The DEP was also closed by the Constitutional Court in 1994, and six DEP deputies were sentenced to fifteen-year prison terms. The new successor party, the Democracy Party of the People (HADEP), contested the 1995 and 1999 parliamentary elections, winning 4.2 percent of the vote in the former and 4.7 percent in the latter. However, due to the 10 percent national electoral threshold, it could not obtain any seats in the Assembly.[41] The HADEP was also closed by the Constitutional Court in 2003 and the new successor party, the Democratic People's Party (DEHAP), received 6.2 percent of the vote in the 2002 parliamentary elections. At its closure, the successor party, the Democratic Society Party (DTP), nominated its candidates as independents in the 2007 elections in order to circumvent the 10 percent national threshold and, thus, was able to elect twenty-one deputies with 5.24 percent of the national vote. The DTP met the same fate as its predecessors, being closed down by the Constitutional Court in 2009. The new successor party, the Peace and Democracy Party (BDP), resorted to the same strategy in the 2011 elections and won thirty-six seats (as independents) with 6.6 percent of the national vote.

Thus, the current Turkish party system still seems to be based on an essentially center-periphery cleavage. The peripheral opposition, however, is now divided into two distinct lines: the religious-conservative peripheral opposition and the ethnic-cultural-geographic (Kurdish) peripheral opposition. The center continues to be represented mainly by the militantly secularist, nationalist, and centrist CHP and its allies within the state establishment. Ali Çarkoğlu and Melvin Hinich argue in the same vein that "very much in line with the center-periphery framework of Mardin, our two-dimensional ideological map reflects pro-Islamist elements of the periphery as opposed to the secularist center as its dominant dimension. Turkish nationalism, defined largely in opposition to rising ethnic Kurdish identity of the late 1990s, appears as a secondary dimension of ideological competition."[42] They also note that "principally as a result of the rise of nationalist and pro-Islamist agendas . . . the appeal of the L-R [left-right] framework has declined. . . . The salience of the constituent parts of the L-R, that is, the distributional economic issues, [and] the role of the state have shrunk in comparison to issues of ethnicity, nationalism and pro-Islamism." They add that, even when the left-right rhetoric was dominant in Turkish political debate as in the 1970s, "instead of a materialist clash between the working masses and the bourgeoisie we see a struggle between a modernizing centrist elite and the conservative parochial forces of the periphery."[43]

In the two-dimensional map of ideological competition in the Turkish party system that Çarkoğlu and Hinich describe, the pro-Islamist party (the FP at the time of their writing) occupies one extreme on the secular-religious axis as opposed to the secularist CHP. The identity-based axis, on the other hand, places the Kurdish parties (the HADEP at the time of their writing) on one extreme and the nationalist MHP and the DSP on the other.[44] The rise of religious- and ethnic identity–based issues should not be interpreted, however, as the weakening of the center-periphery cleavage. Both the religious-conservative opposition and the Kurdish opposition represent different forces on the periphery, and it was precisely these two groups that suffered most under the militantly secularist and nationalist policies of the centrist state.

Here, a note about the ultranationalist MHP is in order. In one sense, the MHP can be characterized as a party of the center because of its strong commitment to Turkish nationalism and statism and its sizable number of supporters within the state establishment. On the other hand, it also shows certain characteristics of a party of the periphery. Indeed, a majority of its voters come from rural areas and lower-middle classes with conservative values. Thus, on the religious-secular axis, it is closest to the position of the pro-Islamist parties.[45]

A variation on the center-periphery cleavage theory is suggested by Ziya Öniş. He sees the present dominant cleavage as one between conservative globalists (i.e., the pro–European Union, pro-EU, forces) and defensive nationalists (i.e., the anti-EU forces). Indeed, Turkey's accession to the EU has recently become one of the most divisive issues in Turkish politics. He thus argues that "a differentiation along the lines of 'globalists' versus 'defensive nationalists' arguably provides a more precise and meaningful distinction in understanding the recent realignment in Turkish politics," particularly in the post-Helsinki era. While many groups within the defensive nationalist camp are broadly supportive of EU membership in principle, they "tend to be uncomfortable with key elements of EU conditionality," which they see as leading to the erosion of national sovereignty and endangering the territorial integrity or the secular and unitary character of the Turkish state. The globalist camp includes moderate Islamists (the AKP), secular liberals, and reformist Kurds whereas the defensive nationalist coalition includes ultranationalists, hard-core Kemalists, and radical Islamists.[46] An interesting paradox in Turkish politics is that a party with Islamist roots has become the leading supporter of accession to the EU and the democratic reform processes associated with it. An equally striking paradox is the increasing alienation of the CHP, the leading protagonist of Westernization and a Western style of life in Turkey, from the objective of EU membership.

However, while accurate, this explanation should not be taken as an alternative to the center-periphery theory, but rather as a qualification to it. Indeed, behind the EU support of two major peripheral groups in Turkish society (the devout Muslims and the Kurds) lies their conviction that their basic rights and interests will be better protected in an EU member country than under a militantly secularist and nationalist, semidemocratic government. In this sense, their support for EU membership is a function of their peripheral position in the society and of their opposition to the center. The anti-EU posture of radical Islamists, on the other hand, can be explained by their total opposition to all Western values.

One of the most cogent criticisms against the center-periphery framework is that both the center and the periphery are subject to change and that they no longer are what they used to be. For example, commenting on the Turkish party system in the mid-1990s, Kalaycıoğlu argues that "the center is no longer what it used to be: Turkey lacks a coherent and compact elite group occupying the center and defending the collective interests of the center."[47] It is true that under the center-right governments, and especially under the AKP government since 2002, many members of the former periphery obtained important positions in the central state machinery. Some observers describe this trend as the "occupation of the center by the periphery." Nevertheless, the cleavage persists in both an ideological and a psychological sense. At present, there is a sharp division between the CHP, the champion of the centrist values, and the AKP, the representative of the periphery, as I analyze in the following chapter.

Notes

1. For this transition, see Ergun Özbudun, *Contemporary Turkish Politics: Challenges to Democratic Consolidation* (Boulder: Lynne Rienner, 2000), pp. 14–24; Ergun Özbudun, *Otoriter Rejimler, Seçimsel Demokrasiler ve Türkiye* (Istanbul: Bilgi Üniversitesi Yayınları, 2011), pp. 117–127; Kemal H. Karpat, *Turkey's Politics: The Transition to a Multi-Party System* (Princeton: Princeton University Press, 1959); Rıfkı Salim Burçak, *Türkiye'de Demokrasiye Geçiş, 1945–1950* (Olgaç Yayınevi, 1979); Mahmut Goloğlu, *Demokrasiye Geçiş, 1946–1950* (Istanbul: Kaynak Yayınları, 1982); Metin Toker, *Demokrasimizin İsmet Paşa'lı Yılları: Tek Partiden Çok Partiye, 1944–1950* (Ankara: Bilgi Yayınevi, 1990).

2. Toker, *Demokrasimizin İsmet Paşa'lı Yılları*, pp. 40–41.

3. Ibid., p. 81.

4. Feroz Ahmad, *The Turkish Experiment in Democracy, 1950–1975* (Boulder: Westview Press, 1977), p. 40.

5. Samuel P. Huntington, *The Third Wave: Democratization in the Late Twentieth Century* (Norman: University of Oklahoma Press, 1991), pp. 174–185.

6. İlkay Sunar, *State and Society in the Politics of Turkey's Development* (Ankara: A. Ü. Siyasal Bilgiler Fakültesi Yayını, 1974), pp. 80–81; also İlkay Sunar, *State, Society and Democracy in Turkey* (Istanbul: Bahçeşehir University, n.d.), pp. 48–55; Ahmet N. Yücekök, *Siyaset Sosyolojisi Açısından Türkiye'de Parlamentonun Evrimi* (Ankara: A. Ü. Siyasal Bilgiler Fakültesi Yayını, 1983), pp. 120–121.

7. See, for example, Robert Bianchi, *Interest Groups and Political Development in Turkey* (Princeton: Princeton University Press, 1984); Metin Heper, ed., *Strong State and Economic Interest Groups: The Post-1980 Turkish Experience* (Berlin: de Gruyter, 1991), esp. chaps. 6, 9, 10, 11.

8. Hakan Yılmaz, "Democratization from Above in Response to the International Context: Turkey, 1945–1950," *New Perspectives on Turkey* 17, no. 3 (1997): 30–31. See also Guillermo O'Donnell, "Delegative Democracy," *Journal of Democracy* 5, no. 1 (1994): 55–69.

9. Frederick W. Frey, *The Turkish Political Elite* (Cambridge: MIT Press, 1965), p. 180.

10. Ersin Kalaycıoğlu, *Turkish Dynamics: Bridge Across Troubled Lands* (New York: Palgrave Macmillan, 2005), p. 74; Tanel Demirel, *Türkiye'nin Uzun On Yılı: Demokrat Parti İktidarı ve 27 Mayıs Darbesi* (Istanbul: İstanbul Bilgi Üniversitesi Yayınları, 2011), pp. 107–130.

11. İlkay Sunar and Sabri Sayarı, "Democracy in Turkey: Problems and Prospects," in Guillermo O'Donnell, Philippe C. Schmitter, and Lawrence Whitehead, eds., *Transitions from Authoritarian-Rule: Southern Europe* (Baltimore: Johns Hopkins University Press, 1986), p. 173.

12. Frederick W. Frey, "Themes in Contemporary Turkish Politics," unpublished paper, Massachusetts Institute of Technology, 1970; Frederick W. Frey, "Patterns of Elite Politics in Turkey," in George Lenczowski, ed., *Political Elites in the Middle East* (Washington, DC: American Enterprise Institute for Public Policy Research, 1975), pp. 79–82.

13. Ergun Özbudun, *Social Change and Political Participation in Turkey* (Princeton: Princeton University Press, 1976), chap. 4. Ergun Özbudun and Frank Tachau, "Social Change and Electoral Behavior in Turkey: Towards a 'Critical Realignment'?" *International Journal of Middle East Studies* 6, no. 4 (1975): 460–480; Ergun Özbudun, "Voting Behaviour: Turkey," in Jacob M. Landau, Ergun Özbudun, and Frank Tachau, eds., *Electoral Politics in the Middle East: Issues, Voters and Elites* (London: Croom Helm; Stanford, CA: Hoover Institution Press, 1980), pp. 107–143.

14. Özbudun, *Social Change and Political Participation in Turkey,* pp. 104–105. Erol Tuncer observes that of ten provinces (constituencies) where the CHP was the first party, seven were in the eastern and southeastern regions (Kars, Van, Hakkari, Bitlis, Bingöl, Erzincan, and Malatya) and the other three (Trabzon, Sinop, and Hatay) were in the Black Sea and Mediterranean regions. The CHP was not the first party in any of the more highly developed Marmara and Aegean regions. Tuncer also notes that the CHP's average vote percentage was the highest in eastern Turkey (50.9 percent, much higher than its national percentage). Erol Tuncer, *1950 Seçimleri* (Ankara: TESAV, 2010), pp. 129–145.

15. Frey, "Themes in Contemporary Turkish Politics," pp. 24–26.

16. Frey, "Patterns of Elite Politics in Turkey," p. 79.

17. On "mobilized participation," see Özbudun, *Social Change and Political Participation in Turkey,* pp. 123, 132–133, 161–163, 169, 182.

18. Joseph La Palombara and Myron Weiner, "The Origin and Development of Political Parties," in Joseph La Palombara and Myron

Weiner, eds., *Political Parties and Political Development* (Princeton: Princeton University Press, 1966), pp. 17–21.

19. Frey, *Turkish Political Elite,* p. 351.

20. Ibid., pp. 352–353, 195–196.

21. Sunar and Sayarı, "Democracy in Turkey," p. 175; see also Tanel Demirel, *Adalet Partisi; İdeoloji ve Politika* (Istanbul: İletişim, 2004).

22. Ahmad, *Turkish Experiment in Democracy,* pp. 251–261.

23. Özbudun, *Social Change and Political Participation in Turkey,* pp. 104–111, 134–137, esp. table 6.2.

24. Özbudun, "Voting Behaviour," pp. 119–135.

25. See, for example, Özbudun and Tachau, "Social Change and Electoral Behavior in Turkey."

26. Ergun Özbudun, "Income Distribution as an Issue in Turkish Politics," in Ergun Özbudun and Aydın Ulusan, eds., *The Political Economy of Income Distribution in Turkey* (New York: Holmes & Meier, 1980), pp. 55–82.

27. Bülent Ecevit, *Atatürk ve Devrimcilik* (Ankara: 1971). Kemal Karpat argues somewhat exaggeratedly that "the deviation of the RPP [CHP] to the left, its rejection of the Kemalist principles, and its espousal of a hodgepodge of minority and potentially explosive causes (for example, Kurdish nationalists found favor with the party) alienated the military from the RPP in general and from Ecevit in particular." Kemal H. Karpat, "Military Interventions: Army-Civilian Relations in Turkey Before and After 1980," in Metin Heper and Ahmet Evin, eds., *State, Democracy and the Military: Turkey in the 1980s* (Berlin: de Gruyter, 1988), p. 148. I show below, however, that the alliance between the CHP and the military was restored in the 1990s and 2000s in the face of the growing power of Islamist-oriented parties.

28. V. O. Key Jr., "Secular Realignment and the Party System," *Journal of Politics* 21, no. 2 (1959): 198–199; see also V. O. Key Jr., "A Theory of Critical Elections," *Journal of Politics* 17, no. 1 (1955): 3–18; see also Walter Dean Burnham, *Critical Elections and the Mainsprings of American Politics* (New York: Norton, 1970).

29. Özbudun, *Social Change and Political Participation in Turkey,* pp. 58–59, 136–137; Özbudun, "Voting Behaviour," pp. 122–135; Sunar and Sayarı, "Democracy in Turkey," p. 183.

30. For limited-choice elections in general, see Guy Hermet, Richard Rose, and Alain Rouquié, eds., *Elections Without Choice* (New York: Wiley, 1978). On the 1983 parliamentary elections in Turkey, see Ergun Özbudun, "Turkey," in Myron Weiner and Ergun Özbudun, eds.,

Competitive Elections in Developing Countries (American Enterprise Institute; Durham, NC: Duke University Press, 1987), pp. 356–361.

31. Üstün Ergüder and Richard Hofferbert, "The 1983 General Election in Turkey: Continuity or Change in Voting Patterns?" in Metin Heper and Ahmet Evin, eds., *State, Democracy, and Military: Turkey in the 1980s* (Berlin: de Gruyter, 1988), pp. 81–102.

32. Ayşe Ayata, "Ideology, Social Bases, and Organizational Structure of the Post-1980 Political Parties," in Atilla Eralp, Muharrem Tünay, and Birol Yeşilada, eds., *The Political and Socioeconomic Transformation of Turkey* (Westport, CT: Praeger, 1983), pp. 32–37. On the ANAP, see also Üstün Ergüder, "The Motherland Party, 1983–1989," in Metin Heper and Jacob M. Landau, eds., *Political Parties and Democracy in Turkey* (London: I. B. Tauris, 1991), pp. 152–169; Ersin Kalaycıoğlu, "The Motherland Party: The Challenge of Institutionalization in a Charismatic Leader Party," in Barry Rubin and Metin Heper, eds., *Political Parties in Turkey* (London: Frank Cass, 2002), pp. 41–61.

33. On the postmodern coup of 28 February 1997, Özbudun, *Contemporary Turkish Politics*, pp. 120–121; Ali Bayramoğlu, *28 Şubat: Bir Müdahalenin Güncesi* (Istanbul: Birey Yayınları, 2001).

34. William Hale and Ergun Özbudun, *Islamism, Democracy and Liberalism in Turkey: The Case of the AKP* (London: Routledge, 2010), pp. 11–16.

35. For an extensive analysis of the ideological differences between the AKP and the so-called national view parties (MNP, MSP, RP, FP), see Hale and Özbudun, *Islamism, Democracy and Liberalism in Turkey*, chap. 2.

36. Ibid., chap. 3; see also Ziya Öniş, "The Political Economy of Turkey's Justice and Development Party," in M. Hakan Yavuz, ed., *The Emergence of a New Turkey: Democracy and the AK Parti* (Salt Lake City: University of Utah Press, 2006), pp. 207, 211–212.

37. M. Hakan Yavuz, "Introduction: The Role of the New Bourgeoisie in the Transformation of the Turkish Islamic Movement," in M. Hakan Yavuz, ed., *The Emergence of a New Turkey: Democracy and the AK Parti* (Salt Lake City: University of Utah Press, 2006), pp. 1, 4–7, 15.

38. Ahmet İnsel, "The AKP and Normalizing Democracy in Turkey," *South Atlantic Quarterly* 102, nos. 2–3 (2003): 297–299.

39. Yılmaz Esmer, "At the Ballot Box: Determinants of Voting Behavior," in Sabri Sayarı and Yılmaz Esmer, eds., *Politics, Parties and Elections in Turkey* (Boulder: Lynne Rienner, 2002), pp. 99–103. Ali Çarkoğlu and Ersin Kalaycıoğlu also describe the changes in the Turkish

party system in the mid-1990s as a "sharp shift to the Right" as "an unprecedented 18 percent registering themselves as 'far right' supporters, and the center of the left-right divide was rapidly eroding." Ali Çarkoğlu and Ersin Kalaycıoğlu, *The Rising Tide of Conservatism in Turkey* (New York: Palgrave Macmillan, 2009), p. 3. Peter Mair argues that "the absorption capacity of left and right now also appears to have accommodated many of the 'new politics' concerns . . . such as issues relating to gender rights, ecology and quality of life. . . . In short, left-right divisions . . . which come to focus principally on the question of the degree of government intervention, have proved sufficiently flexible to endure as well as to absorb, and have thus acted as a fundamental force for continuity." Peter Mair, *Party System Change: Approaches and Interpretations* (Oxford: Clarendon Press, 1997), pp. 26–27. See also Giacomo Sani and Giovanni Sartori, "Polarization, Fragmentation and Competition in Western Democracies," in Hans Daalder and Peter Mair, eds., *Western European Party Systems: Continuity and Change* (London: Sage, 1983), pp. 307–340. Nevertheless, the Turkish perceptions on the left-right dimension still seem exceptional in that they hardly touch on the original economic dimension of the cleavage; namely, the degree of government intervention in economic life.

40. Menderes Çınar, "The Justice and Development Party and the Kemalist Establishment," in Ümit Cizre, ed., *Secular and Islamic Politics in Turkey* (London: Routledge, 2008), pp. 112–120. See also İhsan Dağı, *Turkey Between Democracy and Militarism: Post Kemalist Perspectives* (Ankara: Orion, 2008).

41. On the HADEP, see Aylin Güney, "The People's Democracy Party," in Barry Rubin and Metin Heper, eds., *Political Parties in Turkey* (London: Frank Cass, 2002), pp. 122–137.

42. Ali Çarkoğlu and Melvin J. Hinich, "A Spatial Analysis of Turkish Party Preferences," *Electoral Studies* 25, no. 2 (2006): 370. Other authors also point to the rising prominence of religious and ethnic issues, such as Ayşe Güneş Ayata and Sencer Ayata, "Ethnic and Religious Bases of Voting," in Sabri Sayarı and Yılmaz Esmer, eds., *Politics, Parties and Elections in Turkey* (Boulder: Lynne Rienner, 2002), pp. 137–155; Ayşe Ayata, "The Emergence of Identity Politics in Turkey," *New Perspectives on Turkey* 17, no. 3 (1997): 59–73; and Ersin Kalaycıoğlu, "The Shaping of Party Preferences in Turkey: Coping with the Post–Cold War Era," *New Perspectives on Turkey* 20, no. 1 (1999): 47–76.

43. Çarkoğlu and Hinich, "A Spatial Analysis of Turkish Party Preferences," pp. 370, n. 1, 384.

44. Ibid., p. 378. On the MHP, in general, see Alev Çınar and Burak Arıkan, "The Nationalist Action Party: Representing the State, the Nation, or the Nationalists?" in Barry Rubin and Metin Heper, eds., *Political Parties in Turkey* (London: Routledge, 2002), pp. 25–40; Ziya Öniş, "Globalization, Democratization and the Far Right: Turkey's Nationalist Action Party in Critical Perspective," *Democratization* 10, no. 1 (2003): 27–52; Jacob M. Landau, *Radical Politics in Modern Turkey* (Leiden: E. J. Brill, 1974), chap. 6.

45. Çarkoğlu and Hinich, "A Spatial Analysis of Turkish Party Preferences," p. 378.

46. Ziya Öniş, "Conservative Globalists Versus Defensive Nationalists: Political Parties and Paradoxes of Europeanization in Turkey," *Journal of Southern Europe and the Balkans* 9, no. 3 (2007): 250. See also Çarkoğlu and Kalaycıoğlu, *Rising Tide of Conservatism in Turkey,* pp. 128–129.

47. Ersin Kalaycıoğlu, "Elections and Party Preferences in Turkey: Changes and Continuities in the 1990s," *Comparative Political Studies* 27, no. 4 (1994): 407. For a comprehensive criticism of the center-periphery framework, see also F. Michael Wuthrich, "Paradigms and Dynamic Change in the Turkish Party System" (PhD dissertation, Bilkent University, 2011), chap. 4.

4

The Three Maladies: Fragmentation, Volatility, and Polarization

FRAGMENTATION, VOLATILITY, AND POLARIZATION HAVE been characterized as the "three maladies" of the Turkish party system from the 1970s through the 1990s.[1]

Fragmentation

In the 1946–1960 period, the Turkish party system unquestionably conformed to a two-party model. The two main competitors were the DP and the CHP; the rest of the parties did not satisfy Giovanni Sartori's criteria for "relevance." Sartori defines the "relevance" of a minor party for the party system on the basis of two criteria. One is the party's "governing potential" or "coalition potential." Thus, "a party may be small but have a strong coalition-bargaining potential. Conversely, a party may be strong and yet lack coalition-bargaining power."[2] The second criterion is a party's "intimidation or blackmail potential." In other words, "a party *qualifies for relevance* whenever its existence, or appearance, affects the tactics of party competition and particularly when it alters the *direction* of the competition—by determining a switch from centripetal to centrifugal competition . . . of the governing-oriented parties."[3]

Thus, none of the minor parties in the 1946–1960 period satisfied either of these two criteria for relevance. The total percentage of votes for the two major parties (the DP and CHP) was 94.8 percent in 1950, 93.0 percent in 1954, and 89.0 percent in 1957. Similarly, these two parties together controlled 99.6 percent of the Assembly seats in 1950, 98.5 percent in 1954, and 98.8 percent in 1957.[4] Although some authors argue that fragmentation in the party system began in the 1957 elections,[5] it was an extremely negligible phenomenon since the two minor parties (the Republican Nation Party, CMP; and the Freedom Party, HürP) obtained only 7.1 percent and 3.8 percent of the vote, respectively, and won only four seats each in the home provinces of their respective party leaders (Osman Bölükbaşı and Fethi Çelikbaş) (Table 4.1).

Instead, the fragmentation in the party system actually began with the elections of 1961, under the impact of two extraneous factors. One was the military coup of 27 May 1960, which ousted the

Table 4.1   Vote and Seat Shares for Parties, 1950, 1954, and 1957

Party	1950	1954	1957
DP	52.7	57.6	47.9
	(85.2)[a]	(92.8)	(69.6)
CHP	39.4	35.4	41.1
	(14.2)	(5.7)	(29.2)
MP/CMP/CKMP	3.1	4.9	7.1
	(0.2)	(0.9)	(0.6)
HürP	—	—	3.8
			(0.6)
Effective number of parties (according to vote shares)	2.22	2.17	2.50

Source: Official election results, State Institute of Statistics, from Erol Tuncer, *Osmanlı'dan Günümüze Seçimler, 1877–1999* (Ankara: TESAV, 2002), pp. 321–323.

Notes: a. Figures in parentheses show the percentages of parliamentary seats.

DP, Democrat Party; CHP, Republican People's Party; MP, Nation Party; CMP, Republican Nation Party; CKMP, Republican Peasant Nation Party; HürP, Freedom Party.

DP government and banned the party. The second was the adoption of a proportional representation system by the Constituent Assembly, created by the military government, to take the place of the simple plurality system with party lists that had been used in all elections during the 1946–1960 period. The closure of the DP created confusion in the minds of its former voters. Thus, in the 1961 elections, three parties competed for their votes: the AP, New Turkey Party (YTP), and CKMP, with 34.8 percent, 13.7 percent, and 14.0 percent of the votes, respectively. The CHP received 36.7 percent of the votes, somewhat below its performance in the 1957 elections. Thus, four parties were represented in the National Assembly of 1961–1965, but the number of parties rose to six in 1965, eight in 1969, seven in 1973, and six in 1977 (Table 4.2).

Obviously, the degree of fragmentation in a party system, or the effective number of parties, cannot be measured simply by the number of parties represented in parliament. What is needed is a measure that is sensitive both to the number of parties represented in parliament and to the relative distribution of party shares. Douglas Rae proposes such an index, which can be written as follows:

$$F_e = 1 - \left(\sum_{i=1}^{n} T_i^2 \right)$$

In this equation, T refers to each party's decimal share of the vote. The index value ranges from 0 to 1, with 0 indicating non-fractionalization as in a perfect one-party system and 1 indicating complete fractionalization, "an event never occurring in reality or the formula."[6] The index can be used to measure the fragmentation of both votes and seats. A variation of this formula, as proposed by Markku Laakso and Rein Taagepera, gives the "effective number of parties," which can be written as follows:[7]

$$P_e = \frac{1}{\sum_{i=1}^{n} P_i^2}$$

Using these measures, the index of fractionalization of the National Assembly seats was found to be 0.71 in 1961, 0.63 in 1965, 0.70 in 1969, 0.77 in 1973, and 0.68 in 1977. Similarly, the

effective number of parliamentary parties was 3.3 in 1961, 2.6 in
1965, 2.3 in 1969, 3.3 in 1973, and 2.5 in 1977 (Table 4.2). Since
the AP established itself as the principal heir to the DP, it won
52.9 percent of the vote in 1965 and 46.5 percent in 1969, and
was able to form a single-party government from 1965 until 1971

Table 4.2   Vote and Seat Shares for Parties, 1961–1977

Party	1961	1965	1969	1973	1977
CHP	36.7	28.7	27.4	33.3	41.4
	(38.4)[a]	(29.8)	(31.8)	(41.1)	(47.3)
AP	34.8	52.9	46.5	29.8	36.9
	(35.1)	(53.3)	(56.9)	(33.1)	(42.0)
CKMP/MP	14.0	6.3	3.2	0.6	—
	(12.0)	(6.9)	(1.3)	(0.0)	—
YTP	13.7	3.7	2.2	—	—
	(14.4)	(4.2)	(1.3)	—	—
TİP	—	3.0	2.7	—	0.1
		(3.3)	(0.5)		(0.0)
MHP	—	2.2	3.0	3.4	6.4
		(2.5)	(0.2)	(0.7)	(3.6)
GP/CGP	—	—	6.6	5.3	1.9
			(3.3)	(2.9)	(0.7)
TBP	—	—	2.8	1.1	0.4
			(1.8)	(0.2)	(0.0)
DemP	—	—	—	11.9	1.9
				(10.0)	(0.2)
MSP	—	—	—	11.8	8.6
				(10.7)	(5.3)
Effective number of parties	3.3	2.6	2.3	3.3	2.5
Index of fractionalization (according to their percentage of votes)	0.71	0.63	0.70	0.77	0.68

Source: Official election results, State Institute of Statistics, from Erol Tuncer,
Osmanlı'dan Günümüze Seçimler, 1877–1999 (Ankara: TESAV, 2002), pp.
324–328.
Notes: a. Figures in parentheses show the percentages of seats in the National
Assembly.
   CHP, Republican People's Party; AP, Justice Party; CKMP, Republican Peasant
Nation Party; MP, Nation Party; YTP, New Turkey Party; TİP, Turkish Labor Party;
MHP, Nationalist Action Party; GP, Reliance Party; CGP, Republican Reliance Party;
TBP, Turkey's Unity Party; DemP, Democratic Party; MSP, National Salvation Party.

when the government was forced to resign by a memorandum of high military commanders. Consequently, in these two legislative terms, the effective number of parties fell to 2.6 and 2.3, respectively. The rise in the number of parties represented in parliament was also due to the effects of the proportional representation.

Particularly in the 1965 elections that were held under a national remainder system, which is the most proportional version of the proportional representation systems, the two ideological minor parties (the TİP and MHP) were able to send some deputies to the National Assembly, with 3.3 percent and 2.2 percent of the vote, respectively. With the change to the less proportional d'Hondt system in the 1969 elections, however, their number of seats dwindled to two and one, respectively. Another minor party that appeared in the 1969 elections was the Turkey's Unity Party (TBP). The TBP represented the Alevis (a minority heterodox Muslim sect), which up to that time had regularly supported the CHP. The TBP won 1.8 percent of the seats with 2.8 percent of the votes. However, in elections that followed in 1973, its percentage of votes fell to 1.1 percent and its number of seats to one because most Alevis returned to the CHP fold.

In the confused political atmosphere of the semimilitary regime of 1971–1973, a split took place within the ranks of the center-right: a group of deputies broke from the AP and formed the Democratic Party (DemP). The DemP contested the 1973 elections and won a sizable proportion (10 percent) of the Assembly seats with 11.9 percent of the national vote. Its votes fell sharply, however, in the 1977 elections to 1.9 percent with a single parliamentary seat. A more permanent split took place with the formation of the Islamist MNP; later, the MSP. The party obtained 11.8 percent of the vote and 10.7 percent of the seats in the 1973 elections. In the 1977 elections, with some decline in its popularity, it won 5.3 percent of the seats and 8.6 percent of the votes (Table 4.2).

The Turkish party system in the 1961–1980 period seems to conform to Sartori's moderate multiparty system in its format, but not in its functional or mechanical properties. Indeed, Sartori identified two subtypes of multiparty systems; namely, "moderate" pluralism and "extreme" or "polarized" pluralism. By format, he refers to the number of relevant parties in the system. Thus, he argues, "when party systems are classified according to the numerical criterion, they are classified on the basis of their *format*—how many parties they contain. But the format is interesting only to the extent that it affects the *mechanics*—how the system works. In other words, the format is interesting only to the extent that it contains *mechanical* predispositions, that it goes to determine a set of functional properties of the party system first, and of the overall political system as a consequence."[8] With regard to the format, Sartori argues that the demarcation line between the two types is between five and six relevant parties.[9] The mechanical criterion, on the other hand, refers to the ideological distance among relevant parties. Thus, he argues that moderate pluralism "is characterized by (i) a relatively small ideological distance among its relevant parties, (ii) a bipolar coalitional configuration, and (iii) centripetal competition."[10] An extreme multiparty system, on the other hand, is characterized by the presence of relevant anti-system parties, bilateral (mutually exclusive) oppositions, the occupation of the center by one party or a group of centrist parties (i.e., the only parties with a capability to govern), polarization, a centrifugal drive, and the "politics of outbidding."[11]

Bipolar configuration in a moderate multiparty system refers to the existence of two alternative coalitions instead of two parties. Therefore, alternation in government usually takes place between these two blocs of parties, which leads them to adopt more pragmatic and responsible policies. As a consequence, the direction of the competition is centripetal since both blocs or coalitions aim at capturing the centrist voters, as in the case of a two-party system.[12]

Thus, with regard to the format, the Turkish party system in the 1961–1980 period was closer to moderate multipartism. In the 1961–1965 parliament, there were four relevant parties and essentially two alternative coalitions: one was formed around the CHP, and the other was a center-right coalition formed by the three successor parties to the DP (the AP, YTP, and CKMP). The first model was imposed by the departing armed forces; it led to three short-lived and unstable coalition or minority governments under the premiership of the CHP leader, İsmet İnönü. With the waning possibility of an open military intervention, in 1964 a center-right coalition government was formed. The period from 1965 to 1971 was one of single-party government by the AP, which won an absolute majority of seats in the 1965 and 1969 elections.

The 1973 elections that marked the end of the semimilitary rule of 1971–1973[13] created a more complicated picture. As mentioned above, this period witnessed the fragmentation of the center-right with the emergence of the DemP and the MNP/MSP and the rise of the CHP under the leadership of Bülent Ecevit. Despite this fragmentation, the format of the party system remained closer to moderate multipartism. There were essentially four main actors in the 1973 and 1977 Assemblies: the AP, CHP, MSP, and DemP. This meant that there was a possibility for two alternative coalitions: one under the leadership of the AP and the other under the CHP. In fact, both models were tried in this period.

On the other hand, certain characteristics of the party system in the 1973–1980 period bring it closer to extreme or polarized multiparty systems from a functional point of view. One was the rise of the antisystem parties whose commitment to democratic rule was at best dubious. One of these parties was the ultranationalist MHP, which obtained 3.4 percent of the votes in 1973 and 6.4 percent in 1977. It was widely believed at that time that the MHP had organic ties to violent extreme right groups (the so-called Grey Wolves or the Idealists). The other was the Islamist MSP. Although the MSP did not get involved in violent activities, its political discourse contained strong elements incompatible with certain fundamental values of pluralist democracy.[14] If an "antisystem party" is defined as one that "*undermines the legitimacy* of the regime it opposes,"[15] then the MSP (and its successor, the RP) can be characterized as an antisystem party.

An additional factor that further aggravated the situation was the peculiar balance of forces in parliament and the refusal of the two major parties (the AP and CHP) to enter into a grand coalition even in the face of grave threats to the regime. The close division between the two major parties gave the minor parties, including the antisystem ones, the role of the kingmaker or a coalition potential, in Sartori's words. Thus, the MHP obtained two ministerial positions in the 1975 AP-led coalition government while it had only three seats in the Assembly. Similarly, the CHP-led government of

Ecevit, formed on 5 January 1978, contained two ministers from the Republican Reliance Party (CGP) in exchange for three seats in the Assembly, and one minister from the DemP with only one seat in the Assembly, in addition to eleven independents who split from the AP. Throughout this period, the Islamist MSP remained an indispensable coalition partner in both the AP- and CHP-led governments of Süleyman Demirel and Ecevit.

As the experience of many countries has shown, antisystem parties can perhaps be tolerated in opposition, but their coalition partnership in the government tends to place too heavy a load on the system to be handled by democratic means. This was exactly the case in Turkey from 1973 to 1980. The two antisystem minor parties used their enormous bargaining, or blackmailing, power to obtain important ministries and to fill them with their partisans, seriously undermining the efficient functioning of public bureaucracy.

Even more importantly, this situation encouraged the two major parties to engage in "semiloyal" behavior in the words of Juan Linz, who argues that "an indicator of semiloyal behavior, and a source of perceptions leading to questions about the loyalty of a party to the system, is a willingness to encourage, tolerate, cover up, treat leniently, excuse or justify the actions of other participants that go beyond the limits of peaceful, legitimate patterns of politics in a democracy." He continues, stating that parties "may reject the means as undignified and extreme, but excuse them and . . . not denounce them publicly because of agreement with the goals so pursued. Such agreement in principle and disagreement on tactics is a frequent indicator of semiloyalty. . . . Unequal application of justice to the illegal acts of different disloyal oppositions contributes decisively to the image of semiloyalty."[16]

Linz's words accurately describe the situation in Turkey following the retransition to democratic rule in 1973. Both major parties can be said to have become involved in semiloyal behavior. The AP was in coalitions with the two antisystem parties (the MHP and MSP) for most of the period. Therefore, it tended to treat the violent actions of the extremist rightist groups with organic ties to its coalition partner, the MHP, "with leniency" and toleration. Demirel is famous for having said that "nobody can make me say that rightists and nationalists are committing murders."[17] On the other hand, when the CHP led the government, it had no radical leftist partner in parliament. However, many CHP deputies harbored sympathy for the radical leftist, mostly student-based, violent groups. Therefore, neither major party had the political will to act decisively and evenhandedly against violent groups on the extreme left and right. Consequently, the dynamics of the party competition were clearly in a centrifugal direction and the period displayed an intense polarization that is characteristic of extreme multiparty systems, as I discuss below in more detail.[18] The period ended with the military coup of 12 September 1980.

While promising a return to civilian rule, the three-year military rule of the National Security Council regime of 1980–1983 made it equally clear that the NSC did not intend a return to the status quo ante. Indeed, it attempted to radically restructure the Turkish constitutional, political, social, and even economic systems.[19] Particularly relevant to the present purposes, the NSC attempted to redesign the party system according to its own blueprint. Among the most consequential changes that it introduced toward this aim was the adoption of a 10 percent national threshold in parliamentary elections. This was designed to prevent smaller, more ideological, or antisystem parties from gaining representation in parliament. It was also hoped that this measure would radically limit the number of parties represented in parliament. Indeed, General Kenan Evren, the leader of the coup and head of the state during the military rule, often repeated his preference for a two-party or, at most, a two-and-a-half-party system.

A more radical measure was the banning of all political parties that existed on the eve of the intervention as well as the introduction of ten- and five-year bans on the political activities of the leading cadres and parliamentarians of the preexisting parties. This ban was repealed by a constitutional amendment in 1987, which was approved by a popular referendum.

Finally, in the 6 November 1983 parliamentary elections that marked the transition to civilian rule, the NSC permitted the participation of only three parties (as discussed in Chapter 3). This election, however, proved to be a truly surprising election. The ANAP, the party least favored by the military, won an absolute majority of seats with 45.2 percent of the vote while the military's favorite party, the MDP, finished a poor third with only 17.8 percent of the vote. The HP, designed to play the role of a loyal leftist opposition, received 30.5 percent of the vote, well below the CHP vote in 1977. Expectedly, the effective number of parties was only 2.5 (Table 4.3).

As the democratic transition process proceeded, the old parties reemerged under new names and, with the referendum of 6 September 1987, the ban on former politicians was repealed. Consequently, the 1987 elections were held under more normal conditions. The ANAP repeated its victory with a reduced percentage of votes (36.3 percent), but an increased percentage of seats (64.9 percent) thanks to certain changes that it made in the electoral law, as I discuss in Chapter 5. In the meantime, the two parties created by the NSC regime disappeared: the HP joined the SODEP under the name of the Social Democratic Populist Party (SHP), while the MDP dissolved itself and most of its deputies joined the ANAP. Apart from the ANAP, two other parties were represented in the Assembly, the SHP with 24.7 percent and the DYP with 19.1 percent of the vote. The effective number of parliamentary parties fell further to 2.0.

The ANAP's popularity began to wane after the 1987 elections. The DYP established itself as a more credible heir to the AP, and strong competition for the center-right votes emerged between the ANAP and DYP. A similar competition appeared on the center-left between the SHP and the DSP headed by the former CHP leader, Ecevit. Another development was the rapid rise of the pro-Islamist RP. Due to this fragmentation, five parties were able to gain seats in the Assembly (the RP in coalition with two other rightist parties) and the number of effective parties rose to 3.5. Fragmentation continued to increase in the 1995 and 1999 elections, despite the 10 percent national threshold. Thus, five parties were represented in each Assembly and the effective number of parties rose to 4.3 and 4.9, respectively.

In this period, the fragmentation of votes was considerably higher than the fragmentation of parliamentary seats due to the 10 percent national threshold. Thus, the fragmentation of the vote shares of parties as measured by Rae's index of fractionalization rose steadily from 0.66 in 1983 to 0.75 in 1987, 0.79 in 1991,

Table 4.3   Vote and Seat Shares for Parties, 1983–1999

Party	1983	1987	1991	1995	1999
ANAP	45.1	36.3	24.0	19.6	13.2
	(53.0)[a]	(64.9)	(25.6)	(24.0)	(15.6)
HP	30.5	—	—	—	—
	(29.2)				
MDP	23.3	—	—	—	—
	(17.8)				
SHP	—	24.8	20.8	—	—
		(22.0)	(19.5)		
DYP	—	19.1	27.0	19.2	12.0
		(13.1)	(39.5)	(24.6)	(15.5)
RP/FP	—	7.2	16.9[b]	21.4	15.4
		(0.0)	(13.8)	(28.7)	(20.2)
DSP	—	8.5	10.8	14.6	22.2
		(0.0)	(1.6)	(13.8)	(24.7)
MHP	—	2.9	—	8.2	18.0
		(0.0)		(0.0)	(23.4)
CHP	—	—	—	10.7	8.7
				(8.9)	(0.0)
HADEP	—	—	—	4.2	4.7
				(0.0)	(0.0)
Effective number of parties	2.5	2.0	3.5	4.3	4.9
Index of fractionalization (according to their percentage of votes)	0.66	0.75	0.79	0.83	0.86

Source: Official election results, State Institute of Statistics, from Erol Tuncer, *Osmanlı'dan Günümüze Seçimler, 1877–1999* (Ankara: TESAV, 2002), pp. 329–335.

Notes: a. Figures in parentheses show the percentages of parliamentary seats.

b. The RP contested the elections in alliance with the MHP and the Reformist Democracy Party (IDP).

ANAP, Motherland Party; HP, Populist Party; MDP, Nationalist Democracy Party; SHP, Social Democratic Populist Party; DYP, True Path Party; RP, Welfare Party; FP, Virtue Party; DSP, Democratic Left Party; MHP, Nationalist Action Party; CHP, Republican People's Party; HADEP, Democracy Party of the People.

0.83 in 1995, and 0.86 in 1999 (Table 4.3). The increasing fragmentation in the party system testifies to the limited effects of such electoral engineering efforts as designed by the NSC regime.

The period that started with the 2002 elections displayed a tendency in the opposite direction. The AKP, which was established as a successor to the banned RP and the FP, emerged as the victor with 34.3 percent of the votes and 66.0 percent of the seats, and was able to form the first single-party government since 1991. The only other party represented in parliament was the CHP (it now regained its old name) with 19.4 percent of the votes. The AKP repeated its success in the 2007 and 2011 elections, each time increasing its percentage of votes (46.6 percent in 2007 and 49.8 percent in 2011). The effective number of parties was 1.2 in 2002, 1.4 in 2007, and 1.5 in 2011. Similarly, the fragmentation of votes fell from 0.81 in 2002 to 0.72 in 2007 and 0.66 in 2011 (Table 4.4). I discuss below

Table 4.4 Vote and Seat Shares for Parties, 2002–2011

Party	2002	2007	2011
AKP	34.3	46.6	49.8
	(66.0)[a]	(62.0)	(59.3)
CHP	19.4	20.9	26.0
	(32.4)	(20.4)	(24.5)
DYP/DP	9.5	5.4	0.7
	(0.0)	(0.0)	(0.0)
ANAP	5.1	—	—
	(0.0)		
MHP	8.4	14.3	13.0
	(0.0)	(12.7)	(9.6)
SP	2.5	2.3	1.3
	(0.0)	(0.0)	(0.0)
DEHAP/independents	6.2	5.2	6.6
	(0.0)	(4.0)	(6.5)
GeP	7.3	3.0	—
	(0.0)	(0.0)	
DSP	1.2	(0.0)	0.3
	(0.0)	—	(0.0)
Effective number of parties	1.2	1.4	1.5
Index of fractionalization (according to their percentage of votes)	0.81	0.72	0.66

Source: Official election results from the State Institute of Statistics. See also Erol Tuncer, *Seçim 2011: 12 Haziran 2011 Seçimleri, Sayısal ve Siyasal Değerlendirme* (Ankara: TESAV, 2011), pp. 158–159.

Notes: a. Figures in parentheses show the percentages of parliamentary seats.

AKP, Justice and Development Party; CHP, Republican People's Party; DYP, True Path Party; DP, Democrat Party; ANAP, Motherland Party; MHP, Nationalist Action Party; SP, Felicity Party; DEHAP, Democratic People's Party; GeP, Young Party; DSP, Democratic Left Party.

whether this means a transformation of the party system into a predominant party system.

Volatility

Electoral volatility, which refers to the net change within the electoral party system resulting from individual vote switching, is an important measure of party system change. Volatility has become a matter of greater academic attention in recent decades. Indeed, as Ivor Crewe observes, "in the early 1970s the watchwords were continuity, stability and resilience; not, as they are now, change, volatility and erosion. . . . Over the last decade, however, this picture of rock-like stability was increasingly called into question. Fragmentary yet accumulating evidence suggested that party systems were not as impervious to change, the electorate not as staunchly loyal, as they had been in the earlier post-war period."[20]

Electoral volatility is strongly associated with Seymour Martin Lipset and Stein Rokkan's thesis that Western European party systems have been essentially "frozen" since the 1920s.[21] This view is based on the assumption that "party systems and the voting alignments on which they were based were reflections of the country's social structure. . . . Social structures change but glacially . . . hence it was hardly surprising that elections registered continuity rather than change in party systems and their mass base."[22] I discussed whether these assumptions continue to hold true in Chapter 1.[23]

In measuring electoral volatility, a distinction can be made between net volatility and overall or gross volatility. The former, as proposed by Mogens Pedersen, can be calculated as the sum of absolute differences in the party vote percentages between two consecutive elections divided by two.[24] Despite the advantage of its simplicity, however, this index has its own drawbacks, as Crewe points out. Thus, "by giving each party equal weight, whatever its size, it counts the same absolute increment or decrement of votes as equally significant; but one might consider the doubling of a minor party's support from 5 to 10 percent to constitute 'sharper' volatility than a rise from 45 to 50 percent for a major party."[25] Another problem arises from the splitting and merging of parties; namely. whether they should "be added together or counted separately for purposes of comparison with the previous, or following election."[26] Finally, a distinction can be made between interparty volatility and interbloc volatility if parties in the system can be counted as members of a smaller number of blocs or coalitions. In Turkey, for example, interbloc volatility has been much lower than interparty volatility, as I discuss below.

Distinct from net volatility, "overall or gross volatility refers to the total amount of individual vote switching," as Crewe argues.[27] Overall volatility can be measured by large-scale national surveys and, ideally, by panel surveys. Although the two kinds of volatility are interrelated, there is no one-to-one relationship between them.

> Although a substantial amount of net volatility must reflect at least an equally large overall change in individual vote preferences, the reverse does not hold: a small, even zero, net volatility could be the product of considerable, but self-cancelling, change in the electorate. There is no logical reason why net and overall volatility should rise and fall in perfect tandem, indeed there is no predictable relation between them, but in practice roughly parallel movement is the usual pattern.[28]

In the present study, I use Pedersen's index of net volatility not only because of its simplicity, but also because of the inadequacy of the survey data on individual vote switching.

In measuring the net electoral volatility in the Turkish party system, I had to confront the problem of party splits and mergers, as mentioned above. This problem is confounded by military interventions that closed some or all of the existing parties and caused the emergence of new ones under different names. Thus, I computed no volatility index for the 1961, 1983, and 1987 elections. The 1960–1961 military rule closed the DP, and three parties (two of them newly formed) competed for the DP votes in the 1961 elections. Similarly, the 1980–1983 military regime closed all existing parties and only the three licensed parties were able to compete in the 1983 elections. The reason that I excluded the

1987 elections is that the two parties created by the military regime (the HP and MDP) disappeared from the political scene shortly after the return to civilian rule. If they had been included in this analysis, the average volatility index would have been much higher. In calculating the index, I took into account only parties that were able to gain representation in the Assembly in at least two consecutive elections.

I counted separately splinter parties such as the CGP that split from the CHP and the DemP that split from the AP, even though such splinter parties were normally short-lived. The 1991 elections presented a special problem since the RP contested the election in alliance with the MHP and the IDP; however, they split immediately after the elections. Even though the MHP and the IDP deputies were elected on the RP lists, because of the provisions of the Law on the Election of Deputies that did not permit formal electoral alliances, they resigned from the RP immediately after their election and returned to their former parties. Therefore, their vote percentages in the 1989 local elections were taken as a close approximation. In the 1999 elections, the FP was considered a continuation of the RP, which was closed by the Constitutional Court. In calculating the index for the 1991–1995 period, I considered the CHP as a continuation of the SHP. Finally, for the 2002 elections, I treated the AKP and the Young Party (GeP) as the new parties and the SP as a continuation of the FP. Alternatively, if the AKP and SP are both treated as the successors to the FP, the index value falls to 40.6.

Scholars commenting on the Turkish party system in the period from 1961 to 1999 generally point to volatility as one of the three maladies of the party system.[29] Table 4.5 shows both interparty and interbloc volatility index values for the 1961–2011 period. The average volatility index for this period is 19.8.[30] This figure is obviously much higher than in Western European democracies. For example, Peter Mair found that, in 303 elections in thirteen European countries from 1885 to 1985, the overall mean was just 8.6. Furthermore, volatility levels tended "to cluster at quite low values, with more than two-thirds of the cases registering a level below 10, and with just 11 percent registering a level above 15."[31] Similarly, Michal Shamir calculated the average volatility

Table 4.5 Volatility in the Party System, 1961–2011

Years	Interparty Volatility	Interbloc Volatility
1961–1965	24.5	4.5
1965–1969	11.4	3.1
1969–1973	28.4	1.1
1973–1977	18.3	6.8
1983–1987	—	—
1987–1991	15.3	2.1
1991–1995	21.8	1.3
1995–1999	19.8	8.1
1999–2002	53.5	8.7
2002–2007	17.8	2.8
2007–2011	10.2	7.0

index in nineteen democracies from 1840 to 1977 as 11.[32] On the basis of such comparative data, one has to conclude that Turkish electoral volatility is among the highest; in fact, second only to Iceland's score of 23 in Shamir's sample.[33] The Turkish case also differs from the three new Southern European democracies (Spain, Portugal, and Greece), where a high level of volatility was observed immediately following the democratic transition, but fell to lower levels after critical elections and voting behavior became more stable and predictable (excluding, of course, the Greek elections of 2012).[34] A more recent study covering forty-seven democracies and semidemocracies found significant differences between old and established democracies and the newer ones. For example, eight countries whose mean volatility was above 40 were all new democracies where democracy was inaugurated in the late 1980s and the early 1990s: the Philippines, Estonia, Poland, Lithuania, Russia, Romania, Latvia, and Ukraine. On the other hand, all sixteen countries with a volatility score less than 12 were older democracies.[35]

With regard to electoral volatility as an important dimension of party system change, Mair raises a relevant methodological question:

At what point does volatility become important? Do we rate as significant levels of volatility above 5 percent, above 10 percent, or only above 15 percent? Given . . . that total electoral stability is an unreal expectation, what then are the cut-off points beyond which volatility can be seen to reflect meaningful party (if not party system) change? Should such cut-off points be established in absolute terms, or should they be relative to the individual country or period? . . . Even low levels of volatility acquire a degree of significance if they reflect a cumulative trend, in that a sequence of even low volatile elections may create a substantial change in the overall balance of the system. A highly volatile election, on the other hand, may prove relatively insignificant if followed by a second highly volatile election which acts to restore the prior partisan electoral balance.[36]

In analyzing electoral volatility in Turkey, not only the absolute terms but also circumstances specific to the country have to be taken into account, as Mair suggests.[37] In the Turkish case, an important external variable was the military's frequent interventions in politics, which had heavy consequences for the party system. Thus, the 1960 coup banned the DP and the 1980 coup banned all the parties. The semimilitary regime of 1971–1973 was instrumental in the closing of two radical parties (the TİP and MNP). Finally, the soft or postmodern coup of 1997 led to the prohibition of the RP (and, later, the FP) and to the emergence of a new configuration in the conservative periphery. No doubt, such interventions produced a level of volatility much higher than what would have occurred in their absence. Military interventions affected party system stability not only by the banning of certain parties, but also by causing splits within the major parties. Thus, throughout the 1980s and 1990s, the center-right tendency was divided between the ANAP and DYP, and the center-left between the CHP and DSP.

Frequent party splits and the formation of new parties, even when they were short-lived, contributed to high levels of volatility. Table 4.5 shows that the highest scores of volatility (above 20) were recorded in the 1965, 1973, 1995, and 2002 elections: 24.5, 28.4, 21.8, and 53.5, respectively. The high level of volatility in 1965 was due to the rapid erosion of the two successor parties to the DP (the YTP and CKMP) and the rise of the AP as its established heir. Volatility in the 1973 elections was caused by the rise of the CHP on the one hand, and the split of the DemP and the MNP from the AP on the other. Thus, a strong correlation (0.446) was found between the DemP vote in 1973 and the AP vote in 1969 and 1973, meaning that a majority of the DemP voters were former AP voters.[38] In fact, most of them returned to the AP fold in the 1977 elections, as the party's percentage of votes fell from 11.9 percent to 1.9 percent while that of the AP rose to 36.9 percent from 29.8 percent. The high level of volatility in the 1995 elections can be explained by the rapid rise of the RP and the parallel decline of the two center-right parties, the ANAP and DYP. Finally, the incredibly high volatility score (53.5) in 2002 was due to the rise of two new parties (the AKP and, to a much lesser extent, the GeP) and the equally dramatic erosion of three old major parties (the ANAP, DYP, and DSP).

In general, an inverse correlation is assumed between high levels of electoral volatility and party system institutionalization. Scott Mainwaring argues, for example, that democracy can survive with weakly institutionalized party systems, but weak institutionalization damages the quality of democracy and the hopes of its institutionalization.[39] Scott Mainwaring and Edurne Zoco further argue that

> in systems with high volatility party labels provide weaker programmatic cues. . . . Citizens are less likely to be able to identify what the parties are and where they stand, with adverse consequences for programmatic representation. . . . Persistent high volatility introduces more incertainty regarding electoral outcomes and it probably weakens some democratic regimes. . . . Political outsiders come to power more easily. Political actors are less certain about the parameters of the game. . . . It alters elite strategic calculations in presenting candidates for political office and citizens' strategic voting behavior.[40]

However, these negative consequences are associated with only one type of electoral volatility. If volatility is caused by a weakening of the parallelism between the cleavage structure and the party system of a country or the weakening of party identification ties, then we may speak about the deinstitutionalization of the party system together with all of the associated negative consequences. On the other hand, high volatility in one or a few consecutive elections may be the reflection of a realignment in the party system and, therefore, may lead to a higher level of institutionalization. Such is the case in the extremely high level of volatility in the 2002 elections. This marked the beginning of a new secular realignment in the party system and a trend toward a predominant party system, as I discuss below.

In contrast, the high levels of volatility in the 1980s and the 1990s seem to be associated with a general weakening of party identification ties and the increase in the percentage of "floating voters." Thus, Sabri Sayarı, for example, argues that

> emotional attachments formed by voters toward specific parties in Turkey have loosened since the beginning of multiparty politics. The repeated interruptions of electoral politics . . . have not contributed to the strengthening of ties between parties and voters. The volatility of the parties themselves—their disappearance and re-emergence under new names—has created problems for the continuity of party identifications. . . . It is also possible to suggest that there is a linkage between the weakening of the party organizations and a decline of party identification.[41]

In general, there is a clear correlation between weak party identification ties and high levels of volatility. Thus, in his study of the 1991 and 1995 parliamentary and 1994 local elections, Ali Çarkoğlu observes that volatility was higher in the eastern and southeastern regions where the personal influence of candidates and patron-client relationships weigh more heavily.[42]

Studies on electoral volatility in Turkey supports the findings of comparative research to the effect that volatility is lower in the votes of those parties that have stronger roots in the cleavage system of the country.[43] For example, a study conducted by the Public Opinion Research and Consultancy Company (KONDA) prior to the July 2007 parliamentary elections showed that the parties most successful at maintaining their electorates over time were those that reflected social cleavages most closely; namely, the religiously inspired conservative AKP, the ultrasecularist CHP, the ultranationalist MHP, and the Kurdish nationalist DEHAP/independents. Thus, 72.6 percent of those who voted for the AKP in the 2002 elections expressed their intention to vote for the same party in 2007, as did 71.1 percent for the MHP, 79.4 percent for the DEHAP, and 75.5 percent for the CHP. In contrast, volatility was much higher for parties that were not clear reflections of the cleavage structure: the DP/DYP at 47.9 percent and the GeP at 35.3 percent.[44]

Yasushi Hazama, who conducted a comprehensive study of electoral volatility in Turkey, distinguishes two types of volatility. One is related to changes in the cleavage structure as discussed above. The other, which he calls an "economic" or "retrospective" voting model, refers to the voting decisions of individuals

> based on the previous socioeconomic gains/losses under the incumbent government rather than what the government promises. . . . Since cleavage-type and retrospective-type volatilities are subject to different kinds of mechanisms and as their rise and decline are not significantly associated if the overlaps are controlled for, it would be more meaningful to separately analyze two groups of dependent variables—cleavage-type volatilities . . . and retrospective-type volatilities.[45]

Hazama, adopting Stefano Bartolini and Peter Mair's definition of a cleavage as formed by groups that share sociodemographic attributes, collective identity, and organizational expression,[46] distinguishes three types of cleavages in the post-1980 period: secular-religious, Turkish-Kurdish, and Sunni-Alevi. He also studied the effects of these cleavages on the left-right and systemic volatility: "Left-right volatility consists of absolute net vote swings between the votes for the left- and the right-wing parties" while "systemic volatility is comprised of absolute vote swings between the pro-systemic parties and potentially anti-systemic parties. Potentially anti-systemic parties in Turkey include pro-Islamic, nationalistic, and pro-Kurdish parties."[47] Hazama thus concludes that three major social cleavages in Turkey on the whole have increased rather than reduced cleavage-type volatility during the last four decades: (1) Sunni religiosity raised systemic volatility and (2) Kurdish ethnicity raised both left-right and systemic volatilities while (3) Alevi sectarianism reduced left-right volatility. . . . Although the 1980 military intervention aborted the earlier development of a party-cleavage nexus during the pre-1980 period, the post-1980 period has witnessed a stabilization of the relationship between cleavages and political parties, especially since the late 1990s. In other words, social cleavages and the party system in Turkey seem to be heading for convergence.[48]

Developments since 2002 have corroborated Hazama's observations. The current Turkish party system displays an essentially four-party format. The AKP firmly occupies the peripheral or conservative end of the religious-secular axis while the CHP is placed on the ultrasecularist end. With regard to the ethnic (or Turkish-Kurdish) cleavage, the end points are occupied by the ultra-Turkish nationalist MHP and the Kurdish nationalist BDP. The Sunni-Alevi cleavage does not seem to play a major role in electoral volatility since a strong majority of the Alevis consistently vote for the CHP.

The convergence of social cleavages and the party system leaves retrospective or economic voting as the major source of electoral volatility. Thus, Hazama argues that

deep social cleavages increased electoral volatility in the past, but since the 1990s, they have begun to stabilize voting behavior. The party system in Turkey has thus recently anchored into its major social cleavages. . . . In sum, the apparent instability in the party system stemmed not from a lack of representation in parliament of major social groups but from the poor performance of the government. . . . Voters punished the incumbent according to the most recent economic performance prior to a general election. Thus, the worse the economic conditions prior to the election, the greater the loss of votes for the incumbent party/parties.[49]

Indeed, studies on recent Turkish elections have supported the observation that a major part of electoral volatility is due to economic or retrospective voting. Perhaps the most dramatic example of this trend was the 2002 elections when the voters severely punished the three coalition parties (the DSP, ANAP, and MHP), which they saw as being responsible for the grave economic crisis of 2001. All three parties failed to pass the 10 percent national threshold, and the first two entered an extinction process. On the other hand, the AKP's rising share of votes in the 2007 and 2011 elections seems to be closely associated with the AKP government's successful economic performance and the rising levels of economic welfare. For example, Ersin Kalaycıoğlu observes that

> it seems as if the current AKP voters are inclined to identify with the AKP on cost-benefit calculations based upon satisfaction with the performance of the macroeconomic indicators under the AKP government of 2002–2007. Thus, the AKP election victory seems to be less influenced by ideological factors, such as the left-right spectrum, but more from improvement in economic growth and the rapid decrease in the three decades long, stable high consumer price inflation under AKP rule in Turkish polities. Such cultural factors as religiosity and ethnic identity seemed to play a relatively minor role in determining the voters' choice for the AKP.[50]

Çarkoğlu reaches similar conclusions on the basis of his study on the 2007 elections, in which he attempts to determine the effects of retrospective and prospective sociotropic evaluations (i.e., individuals' subjective judgments about the state of the entire country's economic conditions) of their voting decisions. He concludes that

> retrospective sociotropic evaluations have the largest and most persistent impact on most party choice decisions. . . . The most important implication of these findings concerns the dependence of the AKP upon favorable economic conditions or the favorable economic performance of the AKP government. The fact that economic pragmatism appears more significant than

ideological predispositions, especially for the AKP constituency, might be good news for Turkish democracy.[51]

Polarization

Among the three maladies of the Turkish party system, polarization is perhaps the most serious and persistent. Indeed, as shown above, fragmentation and volatility have decreased considerably since the 2002 elections. Polarization, on the other hand, continues to be a distinguishing feature of the Turkish party system.

In this study, the term "polarization" is not used simply in the ideological sense; namely, an increase in the ideological distance among political parties. For many years, Turkish political scientists have attempted to measure such distance on the basis of the voters' self-placement on a left-right axis, and I expressed my reservations about the usefulness of this approach in the Turkish case in Chapter 3. Indeed, even a cursory look at Turkish political history suggests that polarization has been extremely high in certain periods when the ideological gap between at least the major parties was not deep. One particularly good example is the 1950–1960 period when ideological differences between the DP and the CHP were not great, as shown below. Similarly, at the height of the left-right polarization in the 1970s, the ideological differences between the AP and CHP were not deep enough to preclude the possibility of a grand coalition of these two major parties in the face of a grave threat to the democratic regime. Indeed, such a coalition was proposed by many influential NGOs, the military, and a large part of the public, but was not realized because of the calculations of short-term political gains by the leading cadres of both parties.[52] Similarly, at present, the high level of polarization seems to be due less to ideological than to cultural and psychological factors.

Arguably, the roots of such polarization can be found in the deep cultural and psychological alienation between the center and the periphery. In more recent decades, this cleavage has been compounded by the addition of the ethnic (Turkish-Kurdish) and sectarian (Sunni-Alevi) cleavages, neither of which can be properly understood in a left-right paradigm. Thus, many studies have counted Kurdish ethnic parties on the extreme left, depending on the self-placement of their voters. While their leadership at times used a leftist rhetoric, such parties also receive considerable support from religious and conservative Kurds. According to Çarkoğlu's interesting findings, in the 2007 elections there was not much difference among the AKP, MHP, and Kurdish (independent) voters in their religious beliefs and practices and their degree of support for a sharia-based state.[53] Similarly, the Alevi voters' self-placement on the left is due less to ideological commitments than to a historical and psychological attachment to the secularist CHP, which they perceive as a shield against a Sunni-dominated system. Indeed, Çarkoğlu demonstrates that the probability of the Alevis' voting for the CHP was four times higher than the probability of their voting for the other parties.[54]

On the basis of these findings, Çarkoğlu concludes that "ethnic and sectarian backgrounds of individuals consistently appear significant in differentiating people's self-placements along the L-R scale. Those individuals who are of Kurdish ethnic background or who show signs of Alevism are relatively more left-wing. . . . Minority identity affiliations are associated more with left-wing orientations than right-wing ones."[55] He also questions the commonly agreed diagnosis that there is "a continual shift towards the right end of the spectrum in Turkey." His analysis "reveals that a rich array of determinants shape the likelihood of self-placement of individuals along the L-R dimension. . . . The left and the right as reflected in the determinants along the L-R scale have no tangible socioeconomic basis such as economic deprivation but have instead bases in the ethnic and sectarian differences."[56]

Since the self-placement of voters on a left-right scale is not a reliable indicator of political polarization in the Turkish case, a more meaningful measure may be the percentage of voters who refuse to vote for a certain party under any circumstances. According to a study on the 2007 elections by Yılmaz Esmer, 55 percent of AKP voters stated that they would never vote for the CHP under any circumstances, as well as 16 percent of the DTP voters, 12 percent of GeP voters, and 6 percent of MHP voters. Conversely, 60 percent of CHP voters refused to vote for the AKP under any circumstances, but only 14 percent of them refused to vote for the MHP. As Esmer concludes, the most unwanted parties are not the "extremist" parties, but those perceived as more centrist, which is reminiscent of the DP-CHP polarization in the 1950s.[57]

Indeed, the DP-CHP polarization was not based on the deep ideological differences between these parties in either foreign or domestic policies. The CHP's charges that the DP exploited religion, made concessions to the Islamists, and departed from the Kemalist legacy were largely fabricated and exaggerated. The ten-year DP rule did not bring about any changes in the secular character of the government. The removal or relaxation of certain restrictions on the freedom of religion, such as the opening of the imam-hatip schools and the Faculty of Divinity and the introduction of courses on religion on an optional basis, was begun in the last years of the CHP government. However, polarization became extremely high, especially after 1955 when the DP government increasingly resorted to authoritarian measures. In some villages and small towns, the supporters of the two parties even separated their coffeehouses.

Such polarization seems to be due more to psychological than ideological factors. The CHP and the state elites on whose support it depended could not forgive and forget their unexpected loss of power in 1950. Therefore, starting from the first days of the change of government, the CHP pursued an aggressive and provocative policy toward the DP government. The DP, on the other hand, lived in a permanent CHP and especially İnönü phobia, fearing that the former governing party would attempt to incite its supporters to revolt and come back to power by undemocratic means. This fobia led the DP government to resort to antidemocratic measures against the opposition. Thus, in a process of chain reactions, the relations between the two parties came to a breaking point toward the end of the 1950s, and this prepared the ground for the military intervention of 27 May 1960. It is generally accepted that, even though the CHP was not actively involved in the coup, İnönü's statements in the preceding days, such as "when the conditions are ripe, revolution becomes inevitable," "even I cannot save you," and "the Turkish people are no less dignified than the South Koreans" (a reference to the military coup in South Korea that toppled the Syngman Rhee government), provided the final "green light" for it.[58]

The depth of the psychological shock that the CHP experienced as a result of its unexpected defeat in the 1950 elections is revealed by statements of its leading figures. In their opinion, the people made a mistake and would correct it in the next election. For example, Avni Doğan, a leading CHP member, explains that many people voted for the DP in the belief that İnönü would remain president of the republic and out of a desire to have a stronger opposition. A leading, pro-CHP author, Peyami Safa, states in the same vein that, "if there would be an election next week, the DP would not be able to elect even 40 deputies!"[59] It appears that the CHP supporters' naïve "this time it will be different" optimism continues to this day.[60]

Similar observations can be made with regard to the high levels of polarization in the 1970s. Even though the CHP's move to the left under Ecevit's leadership increased the salience of the left-right cleavage in Turkish politics, the ideological differences between the two major parties, the CHP and the AP, remained moderate. The party system's centrifugal dynamics in this period were due more to the coalition or blackmailing potentials of the antisystem minor parties, as explained above. In this critical period, the leadership of both major parties preferred to pursue a polarizing political strategy, one exploiting the fear of fascism and the other that of communism, in order to mobilize their supporters. The result of such polarization was the 12 September 1980 military coup and the breakdown of the democratic regime.[61] The Turkish experience in this period supports Linz's observations that, in many cases of democratic breakdowns, the behavior of major social and political actors played a major role. He thus argues that "the democratic regimes under study had at one point or another a reasonable chance to survive and become fully consolidated, but that certain characteristics and actions of relevant actors—institutions as well as individuals—decreased the probability of such a development."[62]

The period following the 1980–1983 military rule witnessed a marked decrease in political polarization. The ANAP single-party government from 1983 to 1991 followed essentially moderate and liberal policies. After the ANAP lost its majority in the 1991 elections, a reasonably harmonious coalition government was formed between the center-right DYP and the center-left SHP, heirs to the AP and the CHP, respectively. Such left-right coalitions were almost unprecedented in Turkish politics, except for the short-lived CHP-AP coalition in 1961–1962, which was imposed by the departing military and the equally short-lived CHP-MSP coalition under Ecevit in 1974. Even more extraordinary was the three-party Ecevit government from 1999 to 2002, composed of the center-left DSP, ultranationalist MHP, and liberal-conservative ANAP. Such a coalition, which also functioned reasonably harmoniously, would have been utterly inconceivable in the 1970s. Another sign of such convergence is the fact that the comprehensive liberalizing constitutional revisions of 1995 and 2001 were adopted by agreement of almost all parties represented in parliament.[63]

Starting in the 1990s, however, the rise of Islamist and Kurdish parties as described above led to a new wave of polarization. The dominant social cleavages shifted from a left-right axis to secularism–religious conservatism and Turkish nationalism–Kurdish nationalism axes; in both cases psychological factors loom larger than ideological differences in explaining the depth of polarization.

With regard to the secularism–religious conservatism cleavage, the AKP's emergence as the clear victor in the 2002 elections with an almost two-thirds majority in parliament created a shock in the secularist camp similar to the one it experienced in 1950. The secularists perceived the AKP as a radical Islamist party with the hidden agenda of introducing a sharia-based government in Turkey. It is now known that, almost from the beginning of the AKP rule, the armed forces conspired to get rid of the AKP government by illegal means. As of this writing, the conspirators are on trial. The crisis reached a peak point in 2007 on the question of presidential elections. The secularist camp perceived the election of an AKP president of the republic as a grave threat to the secular regime, the capture of "the last citadel of the secular republic." The chief of general staff, Yaşar Büyükanıt, issued a memorandum on 27 April

2007 with the intent of preventing it from happening. And in a ruling of highly dubious legal validity, the Constitutional Court blocked parliament from proceeding with the election of the president. The AKP reacted to this crisis by amending the constitution, with the help of a minor party, the ANAP, to provide for the popular election of the president instead of election by the Grand National Assembly. Following a series of fierce constitutional battles, Abdullah Gül, the AKP's candidate, was finally elected by parliament on 28 August 2007.[64]

Throughout this period, the CHP increasingly moved toward more ultrasecularist positions, apparently condoning and even approving of the military's attempts to oust the AKP government. Thus, the CHP expressed sympathy for the 27 April 2007 military memorandum, as it had done in the case of the 28 February 1997 intervention, and for the Constitutional Court's ruling that effectively blocked the presidential election. In connection with the court proceedings against the members of the military who allegedly were involved in coup attempts (the so-called Ergenekon trials), Deniz Baykal, the former leader of the CHP, declared himself "the defense lawyer of the Ergenekon." Another peak of the crisis occurred when closure proceedings were brought against the AKP by the chief public prosecutor of the Court of Cassation on account of its allegedly antisecular activities. The case was based on flimsy grounds and fabricated evidence. Clearly, the intention was to close the AKP, to ban scores of its leading cadres from political activity for five years, to encourage a split within the party, and to prepare for the formation of an above-party or national coalition government on the model of the 1971 and 1997 interventions. At the end, the Constitutional Court decided not to close the party but to deprive it of half of its state subsidies for one year. In fact, six of the eleven judges voted in favor of closure, but this was just one vote short of the required three-fifths majority (i.e., seven judges). During this crisis, the CHP chose to keep silent, apparently hoping for a closure ruling. Thus, this period can be characterized as one of extreme polarization between the AKP on the one hand and the so-called republican alliance composed of the CHP, the military, and the judiciary on the other. Its repeated electoral defeats created a sense of desperation within the CHP, which prompted it to fight the AKP with the help of the military and the judiciary and, if necessary, by means of dubious democratic legitimacy.[65]

Another round of high tension and polarization occurred in connection with the constitutional revisions of 2010. The revision package, adopted by the AKP majority in parliament and opposed by the opposition parties, involved changes in twenty-three articles and the addition of two transitional articles. The most controversial aspects of the revision package were the changes in the composition and functioning of the Constitutional Court and of the Supreme Council of Judges and Public Prosecutors. The changes were intended to strengthen the democratic legitimacy of these two bodies and to limit their tutelary powers over the political choices of the elected branches of government. Even though the changes were generally in accordance with European democratic standards, the opposition, especially the CHP, criticized them as steps toward making the judiciary a handmaiden of the AKP government. Since the package was adopted by a three-fifths but less than a two-thirds majority, it had to be submitted to a mandatory referendum in accordance with Article 175 of the present constitution. The referendum held on 12 September 2010 approved the package with a 58 percent majority vote.[66]

The current polarization is mainly due to the secularism–religious conservatism cleavage and, as of this writing, it shows no signs of lessening. Even though the AKP governments since 2002 have done nothing to alter the secular character of Turkish political and legal systems, a deep sense of fear and distrust prevails among the secularists who are afraid of the gradual introduction of an Islamic state. This attitude, in turn, can be explained only by reference to the top-down nature of radical secularizing reforms in the early decades of the republic, bordering on an almost hostile attitude toward religion, and the sense of desperation and helplessness of the secularist camp as a result of its repeated electoral defeats.

Another source of polarization in recent decades has been the rise in salience of the ethnic-based cleavage between Kurdish and Turkish nationalists. There has been a wide ideological gap on this issue between the positions of the Kurdish nationalist BDP and the ultra-Turkish nationalist MHP while the two major parties have been placed on a middle ground. However, this issue also displays cultural and psychological, as well as ideological, dimensions. Thus, a 2010 KONDA study shows that 57.6 percent of Turks do not wish to have a Kurdish bride or spouse, 53.3 percent a Kurdish business partner, and 47.4 percent a Kurdish neighbor. Such percentages are somewhat lower among the Kurds, but still considerable: 26.4 percent do not want a Turkish bride or spouse, 24.8 percent a Turkish business partner, and 22.1 percent a Turkish neighbor. The CHP supporters seem to be the most tolerant in this regard, followed by the AKP supporters, and the MHP supporters are the least tolerant, as expected.[67] These findings are supported by those of a 2006 survey, where it was found that 28.2 percent of all respondents did not want to have a Kurdish neighbor. Such percentages are much higher for other "different" categories such as Jews, Armenians, Greeks, atheists, people from a different sect, and homosexuals. The researchers concluded that 36.9 percent of the respondents displayed a high degree of intolerance.[68] Obviously, such cultural and psychological alienation is at least as powerful a factor in polarization as ideological differences on more specific issues. And it is a great obstacle to the peaceful resolution of the Kurdish problem.

The fact that both cleavages involve foundational issues or either/or types of conflicts makes their resolution difficult in the foreseeable future. Thus, Hanna Lerner argues that conflicts involving "competing visions of the state as a whole," usually revolving "around issues of national and religious identity," lead to "an absolute unwillingness to compromise on the issues upon which the conflict is based."[69] Similarly, Albert Hirschman argues that it is easier to settle divisible or more-or-less types of conflicts than nondivisible or either/or ones: "Many conflicts of market society are over the distribution of the social product among different classes, sectors, or regions. Highly varied though they are, they tend to be divisible conflicts over more or less in contrast to conflicts of the either/or or nondivisible category that are characteristic of societies split along rival ethnic, linguistic, or religious lines. . . . Conflicts of the more-or-less type are intrinsically easier to settle than conflicts of the either-or variety."[70]

Changes and Continuities in the Party System

In measuring party system change (and electoral volatility), one must distinguish between volatility among individual parties and volatility across blocs or families of parties. As Mair argues,

> we cannot simply speak of individual parties. Rather, we must be concerned with blocs or families of parties, and with the notion of parties which are cleavage allies as against those which are cleavage opponents. In other words, individual parties do not exist in isolation, but rather form parts of broader political pluri-party political alignments. . . . In one case, the individual party volatilities result exclusively from an exchange of votes between the parties of a given political family while, at the same time, leaving the overall alignment wholly unscathed. In the other case, the individual party volatilities are the exclusive result of an exchange of votes across the broader blocs and thus involve a major shift in the balance of the overall alignment.

Mair adds that, in contemporary West European democracies, "the families have remained stable while their individual members have proved volatile."[71]

Similarly, despite countless changes caused by military interruptions, party closures, splits and mergers, the emergence or disappearance of parties, and a high level of individual party volatility as described above, the Turkish party system displays basic stability. Table 4.6 demonstrates such stability between the left (parties of the center) and the right (parties of the periphery) blocs. Since the transition to a competitive party system in 1946, Turkey has had sixteen general parliamentary elections (excluding the highly controversial 1946 elections). In these elections, the right (peripheral) parties showed a clear superiority, their percentage of votes varying from 55.7 percent (in 1977) to 71.7 percent (in 2007), while the percentage of votes for the left (center parties) varied from 41.4 percent (in 1977) to 26.1 percent (in 2007). The average vote percentages were 63.6 for the right parties and 33.7 for the left parties. In fact, the latter may be lower than what these figures suggest because the Kurdish ethnic parties were

Table 4.6   Total Vote Shares of the Left and Right Parties, 1950–2011

Election	Left	Right
1950[a]	39.9	56.3
1954[b]	35.3	62.3
1957[c]	41.1	58.8
1961[d]	36.7	62.5
1965[e]	30.4	65.1
1969[f]	32.9	61.5
1973[g]	34.4	62.2
1977[h]	41.4	55.7
1983[i]	30.5	68.4
1987[j]	33.2	65.5
1991[k]	31.6	68.0
1995[l]	29.5	68.5
1999[m]	35.7	58.5
2002[n]	28.0	68.1
2007[o]	26.1	71.7
2011[p]	32.6	64.0

Notes: a. Left: CHP; right: DP, MP.
b. Left: CHP; right: DP, CMP.
c. Left: CHP; right: DP, CMP, HürP.
d. Left: CHP; right: AP, YTP, CKMP.
e. Left: CHP, TİP; right: AP, YTP, CKMP, MP, MHP, CGP.
f. Left: CHP, TİP, TBP; right: AP, YTP, MP, MHP, CGP.
g. Left: CHP, TBP; right: AP, MHP, DemP, MSP.
h. Left: CHP; right: AP, MHP, DemP, MSP, CGP.
i. Left: HP; right: ANAP, MDP.
j. Left: SHP, DSP; right: ANAP, DYP, RP, MHP.
k. Left: SHP, DSP; right: ANAP, DYP, RP (in alliance with the MHP and the IDP).
l. Left: CHP, DSP, HADEP; right: ANAP, DYP, RP, MHP.
m. Left: CHP, DSP, HADEP; right: ANAP, DYP, MHP, FP.
n. Left: CHP, DSP, YTP, HADEP; right: AKP, DYP, MHP, GeP, ANAP, SP.
o. Left: CHP; independents (DTP); right: AKP, MHP, DYP, GeP, SP.
p. Left: CHP; independents (BTP); right: AKP, MHP, DYP, SP.
Parties with less than 1 percent of the total valid votes are not included in the calculation.

counted as left parties in this calculation.[72] However, this is a debatable label for those parties. Even though the rhetoric of Abdullah Öcalan, the leader of the Kurdish revolt, contains strongly leftist elements, such parties also receive considerable support from conservative and religious Kurds, as pointed out above. The common bond among their voters is ethnicity- and identity-based claims, not positions on a left-right axis.

Another conclusion that can be drawn from Table 4.6 is the long-term decline in the votes of the left parties. While their percentage of votes varied between 30 percent and 42 percent in the 1950–1980 period, this share has fallen below 33 percent since the 1995 elections. The only exception to this trend was the 1999 election, where the good showing of the DSP was probably due to its increased popularity because of the capture of Öcalan during Ecevit's minority government immediately prior to the elections. Throughout this sixty-year period, the CHP votes exceeded 40 percent only in two elections, those of 1957 and 1977. Both were held under extraordinary circumstances when the future of the democratic regime appeared under severe threat and many moderate voters voted for the CHP out of fear of a breakdown of the regime. Indeed, in both cases, the elections were followed by a regime breakdown. The fact that interbloc volatility has been much lower than interparty volatility is the source of a basic continuity and persistence in the Turkish party system. To put it differently, the Turkish case displays party change rather than party system change, if the latter is defined as the transformation "from one class or type of party system into another."[73]

The Trend Toward a Predominant Party System

The 12 June 2011 general parliamentary elections in Turkey resulted in a clear victory for the governing AKP. The elections were a first in Turkish political history in which the governing party won office in three consecutive elections, each time increasing its percentage of votes (34.3 percent in 2002, 46.6 percent in 2007, and 49.8 percent in 2011). In all three elections, the AKP won close to two-thirds of the seats in the Grand National Assembly, 66 percent in 2002, 62 percent in 2007, and 59.3 percent in 2011. In 2002 and 2011 it nearly doubled, and in 2007 more than doubled, the votes of the second largest party, the CHP. Throughout this period, the effective number of parties ranged from 1.2 in 2002 to 1.5 in 2011. Likewise, the index of fractionalization of votes and the electoral volatility index fell considerably during this period. Thus, the index of the fractionalization of votes was 0.81 in 2002, 0.72 in 2007, and 0.66 in 2011. The volatility index fell from 53.5 in 2002 to 17.8 in 2007 and 10.2 in 2011 (see Tables 4.4 and 4.5).

All of these changes point to a new trend of institutionalization in the Turkish party system toward a predominant party system model. This model has been used by many political scientists, including Maurice Duverger and Sartori. Sartori distinguishes his scheme from Duverger's dominant party concept and conceptualizes it not as a characteristic of a certain party, but as a feature of a "party system." Sartori defines such a system as one in which the major party wins the absolute majority of parliamentary seats in three (or four) consecutive elections. He adds that a party is dominant when it "outdistances all the others" or "it is significantly stronger than the others," and suggests that "about 10 percentage points of difference between the stronger and the other parties suffices to qualify a dominant party."[74] The AKP also qualifies according to these criteria since its electoral victory margin over its closest competitor, the CHP, was about 25 percent in 2007 and about 24 percent in 2011.[75] Thus, under Sartori's criteria, the present Turkish party system qualifies as a predominant party system. It also seems to conform to Jean Blondel's "multi-party system with a dominant party" type.[76]

Of course, the predominant party system is a subcategory of pluralistic party systems. The predominant party's consecutive electoral victories depend on free and competitive elections. Therefore, predominance may end one day so that the party loses office. However, the low probability in the short run of such an alternation in power somewhat changes the dynamics of political competition. With little hope of coming to power, the opposition party (or parties) may resort to more demagogic and less responsible political strategies, to "politics of outbidding" in Sartori's words.[77] The majority party, on the other hand, must follow more inclusive policies to maintain its dominant position. Therefore, it tends to move in the direction of the center.

The 2011 elections confirmed the four-party structure that had emerged from the 2007 elections. It includes the same parties

(AKP, CHP, MHP, and BDP) as represented in the 2007 parliament with the only difference that, at that time, the Kurdish party was called the DTP. However, that party was closed by the Constitutional Court and it reemerged under the name of the BDP. Compared to the 2007 elections, a four-party system seems to have been more solidly established. In 2007, the total vote share of the four parties represented in parliament was 87.0 percent; this rose to 95.5 percent in 2011 despite the 10 percent national threshold. Indeed, many small parties, already on the way toward disappearance in 2007, were almost completely liquidated in 2011, such as the once powerful DSP and the DP that had emerged from the merger of the two once major center-right parties (the ANAP and DYP). Among the parties that remained below the 10 percent threshold, only the SP won more than 1 percent of the vote (1.27 percent). The four parties currently represented in parliament reflect the two basic sociopolitical cleavages described in Chapter 3.

Thus, with the decreasing levels of fragmentation and volatility and the emergence of a four-party system with a dominant party corresponding to the main cleavage lines in Turkey, a trend toward institutionalization of the party system can be observed, in contrast to the deinstitutionalization that was often seen in the 1990s.[78] If as Mainwaring argues, "democracy can survive with weakly institutionalized party systems but weak institutionalization harms the quality of democracy and the prospects for democratic consolidation,"[79] this trend toward party system institutionalization in Turkey augurs well for the prospects of democratic consolidation.

Notes

1. Üstün Ergüder and Richard Hofferbert, "The 1983 General Election in Turkey: Continuity or Change in Voting Patterns?" in Metin Heper and Ahmet Evin, eds., *State, Democracy, and Military: Turkey in the 1980s* (Berlin: de Gruyter, 1988), pp. 84–85; Ergun Özbudun, "The Turkish Party System: Institutionalization, Polarization and Fragmentation," *Middle Eastern Studies* 17, no. 2 (1981): 228–240; Sabri Sayarı, "The Changing Party System," in Sabri Sayarı and Yılmaz Esmer, eds, *Politics,*

Parties and Elections in Turkey (Boulder: Lynne Rienner, 2002), pp. 22–24.

2. Giovanni Sartori, *Parties and Party Systems: A Framework for Analysis* (Cambridge: Cambridge University Press, 1976), p. 122.

3. Ibid., p. 123; emphasis in original.

4. The figures are taken from Erol Tuncer, *Osmanlı'dan Günümüze Seçimler, 1877–1999* (Ankara: TESAV, 2002), pp. 321–323; Erol Tuncer, *1950 Seçimleri* (Ankara: TESAV, 2010), p. 117.

5. F. Michael Wuthrich, "Paradigms and Dynamic Change in the Turkish Party System" (PhD dissertation, Bilkent University, 2011), p. 206.

6. Douglas W. Rae, *The Political Consequences of Electoral Laws* (New Haven: Yale University Press, 1967), pp. 56–57.

7. Markku Laakso and Rein Taagepera, "Effective Number of Parties: A Measure with Application to West Europe," *Comparative Political Studies* 12, no. 1 (1979): 3–27.

8. Sartori, *Parties and Party Systems,* p. 128; emphasis in original.

9. Ibid., p. 131.

10. Ibid., p. 179.

11. Ibid., pp. 131–144.

12. Ibid., p. 179.

13. For this period, Ergun Özbudun, *Contemporary Turkish Politics: Challenges to Democratic Consolidation* (Boulder: Lynne Rienner, 2000), pp. 33–35.

14. William Hale and Ergun Özbudun, *Islamism, Democracy and Liberalism in Turkey: The Case of the AKP* (London: Routledge, 2010), pp. 7–9. This also applies to its successor, the RP.

15. Sartori, *Parties and Party Systems,* p. 133.

16. Juan J. Linz, *The Breakdown of Democratic Regimes: Crisis, Breakdown, and Reequilibration* (Baltimore: Johns Hopkins University Press, 1978), pp. 32–33.

17. *Cumhuriyet* (Istanbul daily), 25 December 1978.

18. Özbudun, *Contemporary Turkish Politics,* pp. 35–43.

19. On the characteristics of the NSC rule, see ibid., pp. 24–28. On the authoritarian and tutelarist features of the Constitution of 1982, see Ergun Özbudun, *The Constitutional System of Turkey: 1876 to the Present* (New York: Palgrave Macmillan, 2011).

20. Ivor Crewe, "Introduction: Electoral Change in Western Democracies: A Framework for Analysis," in Ivor Crewe and David Denver,

eds., *Electoral Change in Western Democracies: Patterns and Sources of Electoral Volatility* (London: Croom Helm, 1985), pp. 1, 3.

21. Seymour Martin Lipset and Stein Rokkan, "Cleavage Structures, Party Systems and Voter Alignments: An Introduction," in Seymour Martin Lipset and Stein Rokkan, eds., *Party Systems and Voter Alignments: Cross-National Perspectives* (New York: Free Press, 1967), p. 50. In the same direction, Richard Rose and D. W. Urwin, "Persistence and Change in Western Party Systems Since 1945," *Political Studies* 18, no. 3 (1970): 287–319.

22. Crewe, "Introduction," p. 2.

23. Ibid., p. 5; Ronald Inglehart, *The Silent Revolution: Changing Values and Political Styles Among Western Publics* (Princeton: Princeton University Press, 1977).

24. Mogens N. Pedersen, "The Dynamics of European Party Systems: Changing Patterns of Electoral Volatility," *European Journal of Political Research* 7, no. 1 (1979): 1–26.

25. Crewe, "Introduction," p. 9.

26. Ibid., p. 10.

27. Ibid.

28. Ibid.

29. Ergüder and Hofferbert, "1983 General Elections in Turkey," pp. 84–85; Sayarı, "Changing Party System," pp. 22–24; Özbudun, "Turkish Party System," pp. 228–240.

30. Ali Çarkoğlu computed the average volatility index value for the 1954–1995 period as 21.2. Ali Çarkoğlu, "The Turkish Party System in Transition: Party Performance and Agenda Change," *Political Studies* 46, no. 3 (1998): 544–571.

31. Peter Mair, *Party System Change: Approaches and Interpretations* (Oxford: Clarendon Press, 1997), pp. 67–68.

32. Michal Shamir, "Are Western Party Systems 'Frozen'?: A Comparative Dynamic Analysis," *Comparative Political Studies* 17, no. 1 (1984): 35–79.

33. Çarkoğlu, "Turkish Party System in Transition," p. 547.

34. Leonardo Morlino, "Political Parties and Democratic Consolidation in Southern Europe," in Richard Gunther, P. Nikiforos Diamandouros, and Hans-Jürgen Puhle, eds., *The Politics of Democratic Consolidation: Southern Europe in Comparative Perspective* (Baltimore: Johns Hopkins University Press, 1995), p. 321.

35. Scott Mainwaring and Edurne Zoco, "Political Sequences and Stabilization of Interparty Competition: Electoral Volatility in Old and

New Democracies," *Party Politics* 13, no. 2 (2007): 155–178, esp. table 1, pp. 159–160.

36. Mair, *Party System Change,* p. 67.

37. Ibid.

38. Ergun Özbudun, "Voting Behaviour: Turkey," in Jacob M. Landau, Ergun Özbudun, and Frank Tachau, eds., *Electoral Politics in the Middle East: Issues, Voters and Elites* (London: Croom Helm; Stanford, CA: Hoover Institution Press, 1980), pp. 135–140.

39. Scott P. Mainwaring, "Party Systems in the Third Wave," *Journal of Democracy* 9, no. 3 (1998): 79.

40. Mainwaring and Zoco, "Political Sequences," pp. 157–158.

41. Sayarı, "Changing Party System," p. 24; see also Yasushi Hazama, *Electoral Volatility in Turkey: Cleavages vs. the Economy* (Chiba, Japan: Institute of Developing Economies, 2007), pp. 10–11; Özbudun, *Contemporary Turkish Politics,* p. 79.

42. Çarkoğlu, "Turkish Party System," pp. 547–549, esp. table 1.

43. Stefano Bartolini and Peter Mair, *Identity, Competition and Electoral Availability: The Stabilization of European Electorates, 1885–1985* (Cambridge: Cambridge University Press, 1990), pp. 241–242.

44. KONDA, *Seçim '07: Siyasal Eğilimler Araştırmaları Özet Rapor,* mimeo (18 July 2007), pp. 25–26.

45. Hazama, *Electoral Volatility in Turkey,* pp. 10–13, 30.

46. Bartolini and Mair, *Identity, Competition, and Electoral Availability,* p. 215.

47. Hazama, *Electoral Volatility in Turkey,* pp. 28–29.

48. Ibid., chaps. 6 and 7; quotation is on pp. 78–79.

49. Ibid., pp. 131–132. See also Yasushi Hazama, "Social Cleavages and Electoral Support in Turkey: Toward Convergence," *The Developing Economies* 41, no. 3 (2003): 362–387.

50. Ersin Kalaycıoğlu, "Justice and Development Party at the Helm: Resurgence of Islam or Restitution of the Right-of-Center Predominant Party?" *Turkish Studies* 11, no. 1 (2010): 39.

51. Ali Çarkoğlu, "Ideology or Economic Pragmatism? Profiling Turkish Voters in 2007," *Turkish Studies* 9, no. 2 (2008): 317–344; quotation is on p. 340.

52. Özbudun, *Contemporary Turkish Politics,* pp. 37–43.

53. Çarkoğlu, "Ideology or Economic Pragmatism?" pp. 332–335.

54. Ibid., p. 328.

55. Ali Çarkoğlu, "The Nature of Left-Right Ideological Self-Placement in the Turkish Context," *Turkish Studies* 8, no. 2 (2007): 253–271, esp. p. 263.

56. Ibid., pp. 267–269.

57. Yılmaz Esmer, *2007 Milletvekili Genel Seçimleri Seçmen Davranışı ve Tercihleri Seçim Sonrası Araştırması,* mimeo, p. 17.

58. Özbudun, *Contemporary Turkish Politics,* pp. 29–33; Metin Toker, *Demokrasimizin İsmet Paşa'lı Yılları: Demokrasiden Darbeye, 1957–1960* (Ankara: Bilgi Yayınevi, 1991). On the İnönü phobia of the Democrats, see also Ahmad, *The Turkish Experiment in Democracy, 1950–1975* (Boulder: Westview Press, 1977), p. 37.

59. Tanel Demirel, *Türkiye'nin Uzun On Yılı: Demokrat Parti İktidarı ve 27 Mayıs Darbesi* (Istanbul: İstanbul Bilgi Üniversitesi Yayınları, 2011), pp. 100–101.

60. Alper Görmüş, "Yüzde 20 Seçimden Ümidini Kesti mi?" *Taraf* (Istanbul daily), 8 July 2011.

61. Özbudun, *Contemporary Turkish Politics,* pp. 35–43.

62. Linz, *Breakdown of Democratic Regimes,* pp. 4–5, 10.

63. Ergun Özbudun and Ömer Faruk Gençkaya, *Democratization and the Politics of Constitution-Making in Turkey* (Budapest: Central European University Press, 2009), pp. 34–68.

64. Ibid., pp. 97–103; also Ergun Özbudun, "Why the Crisis over the Presidency?" *Private View* 22 (2007): 48–51.

65. Ceren Belge, "Friends of the Court: The Republican Alliance and Selective Activism of the Constitutional Court in Turkey," *Law and Society Review* 40, no. 3 (2006): 653–691.

66. Özbudun, *Constitutional System of Turkey,* pp. 104–108, 113–114, 147–149.

67. KONDA Araştırma, *Kürt Mesele'sinde Algı ve Beklentiler* (Istanbul: İletişim, 2011), pp. 106–107.

68. Ali Çarkoğlu and Binnaz Toprak, *Değişen Türkiye'de Din, Toplum ve Siyaset* (Istanbul: TESEV, 2006), pp. 46–51.

69. Hanna Lerner, "Constitution-Writing in Deeply Divided Societies: The Incrementalist Approach," *Nations and Nationalism* 16, no. 1 (2010): 70.

70. Albert O. Hirschman, "Social Conflicts as Pillars of Democratic Market Society," *Political Theory* 22, no. 2 (1994): 213.

71. Mair, *Party System Change,* pp. 28–29.

72. Cengiz Çandar, for example, argues that the PKK (Kurdistan Workers' Party, the militant and violence-prone Kurdish organization) is strongly secularist, and that the perceptions of their leading cadres are shaped by Kemalist and Alevi themes. Cengiz Çandar, "PKK Olayı bir Kürt İsyanıdır," *Taraf* (Istanbul daily), 27 June 2011.

73. Mair, *Party System Change,* pp. 51–52, 54–55. Thus, he argues that

> party system change might ocur when, as a result of ideological, strategic, or electoral shifts, there is a transformation of the direction of competition or the governing formula. If, on the other hand, the change simply involves the realignment of the social bases of support, or the emergence of a new set of issue concerns, while leaving the pattern of competition untouched, this might not be considered of major significance—at least in terms of the party system. (p. 52)

74. Sartori, *Parties and Party Systems,* pp. 192–201. Sartori argues that the major party must maintain its absolute majority "for four consecutive legislatures at least" (p. 196), but then relaxes it to "three consecutive absolute majorities" (p. 199).

75. Ali Çarkoğlu, "Turkey's 2011 General Elections: Towards a Dominant Party System?" *Insight Turkey* 13, no. 3 (2011): 43–62, esp. pp. 44–45.

76. Jean Blondel, "Party Systems and Patterns of Government in Western Democracies," *Canadian Journal of Political Science* 1, no. 2 (June 1968): 184–187.

77. Sartori, *Parties and Party Systems,* p. 140.

78. For an example of such observations, see Sayarı, "Changing Party System," pp. 30–31.

79. Mainwaring, "Party Systems in the Third Wave," p. 79.

5

The Electoral System and the Party System

THERE HAS BEEN CONSIDERABLE RESEARCH ON THE effects of electoral systems on party systems. One of the earliest and most influential formulations on this relationship is put forward by Maurice Duverger:

> The general influence of the system of balloting may be set down in the following three formulae: (1) proportional representation encourages a system of parties that are multiple, rigid, independent, and stable (except in the case of waves of popular emotion); (2) the majority system with two ballots encourages a system of parties that are multiple, flexible, dependent, and relatively stable (in all cases); (3) the simple-majority single-ballot system encourages a two-party system with alternation of power between major independent parties.[1]

Duverger admits that "the most decisive influences" on the party system "are aspects of the life of the nation such as ideologies and particularly the socio-economic structure," and that the electoral system "has no real driving power" and its effects "could be compared with that of a brake or an accelerator." In other words, "the multiplication of parties, which arises as a result of other factors, is facilitated by one type of electoral system and hindered by another." That he devotes a large part of his classic work, *Political Parties,* to the effects of the electoral system, however, is an indication of the importance that he attributes to them. Thus, he argues that "the party system and the electoral system are two realities that are indissolubly linked and even difficult sometimes to separate by analysis."[2]

According to Duverger, his generalization that the simple-majority single-ballot system favors the two-party system "approaches the most nearly perhaps to a true sociological law. An almost complete correlation is observable between the simple-majority single-ballot system and the two-party system: dualist countries use the simple-majority vote and simple-majority vote countries are dualist. The exceptions are very rare and can generally be explained as the result of special conditions."[3] Duverger explains this tendency as the result of two factors, one mechanical and the other psychological. "The mechanical factor consists in the 'under-representation' of the third, i.e., the weakest party, its percentage of seats being inferior to its percentage of the poll."[4] After a while, the mechanical factor triggers the psychological factor: "The electors soon realize that their votes are wasted if they continue to give them to the third party: whence their natural tendency to transfer their vote to the less evil of its two adversaries in order to prevent the success of the greater evil."[5]

Duverger's thesis has been criticized from different points of view. First, the example of Great Britain has shown that the simple-majority single-ballot system has not prevented the rise of the Labour and the decline of the Liberal Party. Thus, in time, Labour replaced the Liberals as one of the two major parties. Second, Duverger's thesis is logically inconsistent since the simple-majority single-ballot system can lead to a two-party competition only at the local or the constituency level, but not necessarily at the national level. If a nationally minor party is one of the two strongest parties in a certain region or constituency, the mechanical and psychological factors would not work against it. Therefore, such a system does not prevent the survival of locally or regionally based parties. They may even enjoy a greater advantage than they would have obtained under a proportional representation system. As Giovanni Sartori observes, "a two-party format is *impossible* . . . if racial, linguistic, ideologically alienated, single-issue, or otherwise incoercible minorities (which cannot be represented by two major parties) are concentrated in above-plurality proportions in particular constituencies or geographical pockets."[6]

In contrast to a simple-majority single-ballot system, both the double-ballot majority and the proportional representation systems encourage a multiparty system. In the double-ballot system, minor parties can conclude electoral alliances in the second ballot and, thus, win seats in the legislature. Therefore, argues Duverger, "the phenomena of polarization and under-representation are not operative here, or operate only at the second ballot, each party retaining unimpaired its chances at the first."[7] Clearly, this system punishes antisystem parties since no prosystem party would be willing to enter into an electoral alliance with them. Sartori sees it as a virtue of the system: "An electoral system that does penalize—as the double ballot surely does—the most-distant, i.e., the most-left and most-rightist (extreme) parties, is doubtlessly a system that eminently facilitates governability under adverse conditions. Which is no small merit."[8]

Finally, with regard to the effects of the proportional representation systems, Duverger observes that, under this system, "there is no encouragement to parties with similar tendencies to fuse, as their division does them little or no harm. There is nothing to prevent splits within parties, for the total representation of the two separate factions will not be mechanically reduced by the effect of the vote."[9] Nevertheless, Duverger sees the "multiplying" effects of the proportional representation as "very limited":

On the whole PR [proportional representation] maintains almost intact the structure of parties existing at the time of its appearance. It never has the disintegrating effect that some people claim for it. . . . The multiplying tendency is shown less through the division of old parties than through the creation of new parties: it should be quite clear that these are essentially small parties. Failure to realize this has caused some people to deny . . . that proportional representation has a multiplying effect. Most of the countries where proportional representation has been effectively used took precautions to avoid this rise of small parties. . . . Fundamentally, "full" proportional representation exists nowhere.[10]

Electoral Systems in Turkey

Turkey offers an interesting case in the study of the effects of electoral systems on party systems. Indeed, since the transition to a competitive party system in 1946, it has experienced many electoral systems with very different effects on the party system, even on the functioning of the political system as a whole. A list of electoral systems applied from 1946 to the present in chronological order includes:[11]

- Simple-majority system with multimember constituencies (party lists), 1946–1960
- D'Hondt system with constituency thresholds for the National Assembly elections, 1961–1964, and for the Senate elections, 1964–1965
- Simple-majority system with multimember constituencies for the Senate elections (1961–1964)
- National remainder system for both chambers, 1965–1969
- D'Hondt system with constituency thresholds, 1969–1980
- D'Hondt system with national and constituency thresholds, 1983–1987
- D'Hondt system with national and constituency thresholds, combined with the simple-majority system, 1987–1995
- D'Hondt system with national, but no constituency, thresholds, 1995–present

Clearly, the most radical change in the electoral system occurred in the aftermath of the 1960 military intervention. The electoral system in force before the intervention (1946–1960) combined a simple-majority system with multimember constituencies at the provincial level. Certain populous provinces elected large numbers of deputies, such as Istanbul with twenty-seven seats in 1950, twenty-nine seats in 1954, and thirty-nine seats in 1957, and the party that obtained a simple plurality of the votes won all the seats in such provinces. Obviously, this system produced extremely disproportionate results at the national level. Thus, the DP won 83.8 percent of the seats with 53.3 percent of the votes in the 1950 elections, 93 percent of the seats with 56.6 percent of the votes in the 1954 elections, and 69.5 percent of the seats with 47.7 percent of the votes in the 1957 elections. It is generally agreed that such lopsided majorities in parliament led the DP governments to pursue intolerant and repressive policies toward the opposition, which was a factor in creating a favorable climate for the military intervention.

Throughout these years (1950–1960), the opposition CHP and the other minor opposition parties advocated the adoption of a proportional representation system. Thus, the Constituent Assembly established after the intervention was given the task of preparing a new constitution as well as a new electoral law. The Law on the Election of Deputies adopted the d'Hondt version of proportional representation with constituency thresholds without much debate. The constituency threshold (or electoral quotient) was computed by dividing the total number of valid votes cast in the constituency by the number of deputies to be elected in that constituency. Parties or independent candidates who received fewer votes than the constituency threshold were not assigned a seat in the Assembly. On the other hand, the Constituent Assembly maintained the simple-majority system with multimember constituencies for the second chamber (Senate) elections. Consequently, the 1961 Senate elections produced a much higher level of disproportionality than the National Assembly elections: the AP won 47.3 percent of the Senate seats with 34.5 percent of the votes while the CHP won 24 percent of these seats with 36.1 percent of the votes.[12]

The change from a majoritarian to a proportional representation system was in conformity with the spirit of the new Constitution of 1961. It is generally agreed that this constitution represented a radical change from a majoritarian to a pluralist type of democracy with proper checks and balances on the powers of parliamentary majorities. It has been rightly pointed out that simple-majority single-ballot systems correspond to majoritarian conceptions of democracy while the proportional representation systems are among the principal instruments of a pluralist or consensus model of democracy:

> The typical electoral system of majoritarian democracy is the single-member district plurality or majority system; consensus democracy typically uses proportional representation. The plurality and majority single-member district methods are a perfect reflection of majoritarian philosophy: the candidate supported by the largest number of voters wins, and all other voters remain unrepresented. . . . In sharp contrast, the basic aim of proportional representation is to represent both majorities and minorities and, instead of overrepresenting or underrepresenting any parties, to translate votes into seats proportionally.[13]

G. Bingham Powell Jr. argues in a similar vein that the choice of an electoral system is associated with two conceptions of democracy and of the citizens' role in it. The majoritarian vision, which involves the concentration of policymaking power in the hands of the elected majority, assumes that "one can reasonably identify what citizens want . . . and the problem of elections is to make policy-makers follow that citizen directive. The dispersed power vision tends to assume that citizens are not a homogeneous bunch, and the main problem of elections is to see that everybody and everybody's views get taken into account in policy making."[14] Thus, in 1961, Turkey made a critical choice in favor of a proportional vision. Even though Turkish Electoral Laws have undergone a number of changes since then, the electoral system has always remained some version of proportional representation, as I describe below.

The first such change was made just prior to the 1965 elections. The rapid rise of the AP as the then-established heir to the DP, as shown by its 50.3 percent of the vote in the 7 June 1964 Senate elections, led the other parties (the CHP and two minor parties, the YTP and CKMP) to switch to an even more proportional version of the system in order to prevent the AP from obtaining an absolute majority of seats in the forthcoming National Assembly elections. Thus, a national remainder system, most favorable to small parties, was adopted for both the National Assembly and the Senate elections. However, even this most proportional system could not prevent an AP victory with 52.9 percent of votes and 53.3 percent of seats. An interesting outcome of this change was the entry into parliament of the two minor and highly ideological extreme parties, the Marxist TİP (fifteen seats) and the ultranationalist MHP (eleven seats).

The next change was made by the AP majority in parliament, with the intention of maintaining its majority status in the future elections by giving the major parties a certain advantage. Thus, an amendment to the Electoral Law, enacted on 23 March 1968, returned to the d'Hondt system with constituency thresholds for both chambers. However, the Constitutional Court, in a highly controversial ruling, annulled the provisions of the law related to constituency thresholds.[15] Even though the constitution expressed no choice for a particular electoral system, the court identified democratic elections with a pure form of proportional representation and argued that electoral thresholds constituted an "artificial intervention into the natural flow of the electoral process."[16] Thus, ironically, with the annulment of the provisions on constituency thresholds, the system became the d'Hondt system without thresholds, contrary to the will of the parliament, and it remained in force until the military intervention of 12 September 1980.

The diagnoses of the leaders of the 1980–1983 military regime for the causes of the political crisis in the late 1970s shaped not only its policies for the highly authoritarian and restrictive Constitution of 1982, but also its choice for an electoral system. In the view of the military rulers, the crisis was at least partly due to the excessive fragmentation of the party system and the blackmailing or kingmaker power obtained by the extremist minor parties such as the MSP and the MHP. Therefore, their remedy consisted of a d'Hondt system not only with constituency thresholds, but also with an excessively high national threshold of 10 percent. They hoped that, with the help of the national threshold, they would be able to restructure the party system in a two-party or a two-and-a-half-party system direction. This choice was expressed clearly by General Kenan Evren, the leader of the 1980 coup and the head of state in the interim period:

> In view of the problems we experienced because of coalition governments, I believed that it was necessary to introduce an electoral threshold. The sole problem was to determine the percentage of such threshold. I thought 10 percent would be appropriate, while certain experts proposed 8, 7, and even 5 percent. After long debates, 10 percent was adopted. In my view, the greater the number of parties in parliament, the higher the probability of coalition governments. When we look at the USA and the UK, there are two main parties and other parties are insignificant, and governments do not fall often between the two elections leading to crises. I had a strong desire for a system of two major parties where power alternates between them as in those countries.[17]

The 1983 Law on the Election of Deputies did not limit itself to introducing a double-threshold system, but also reduced the size of electoral districts, or constituencies, which varied from two to seven. This resulted in the division of large provinces into smaller electoral districts. As I show below, there is an inverse correlation between the size of constituencies and the proportionality of the electoral system. Smaller constituencies mean higher constituency-level thresholds and, thus, work against minor parties.

During the ANAP single-party government period, the Electoral Law was changed again in 1986 and 1987 so as to strengthen its majoritarian features and to increase its disproportionality.[18] Thus, the maximum size of electoral districts was further reduced from seven to six. In districts with four or more seats, one deputy would be elected by the simple plurality system. And in the calculation of the constituency threshold in districts with six seats, the number of valid votes would be divided by five instead of six. All of these changes clearly favored the major parties (particularly the strongest party) and further disadvantaged minor parties. Indeed, as a result of such electoral engineering, the ANAP was able to increase its parliamentary majority from 52.9 percent (in 1983) to 64.9 percent (in 1987), despite a considerable fall in its share of votes from 45.2 percent to 36.6 percent. Interestingly, contrary to its controversial 1968 ruling discussed above, these changes were not found unconstitutional by the Constitutional Court. This time, the court correctly observed that the constitution had expressed no choice for a particular electoral system and that it was within the margin of appreciation of parliament to choose an electoral system provided that it did not violate democratic standards.[19]

In 1995, Article 67 of the constitution was amended to stipulate that "electoral laws shall be made in a way to reconcile the principles of fairness in representation and stability in government." Since these two objectives are clearly contradictory, the meaning of this amendment can only be that the constitution does not permit pure majoritarian or pure proportional systems, but that it is open to many kinds of mixed systems to be freely decided by the legislature. On the other hand, this formulation leaves a considerable margin of appreciation to the Constitutional Court on the proper nature of this mix. Another constitutional amendment made in 2001 stipulated that changes made in Electoral Laws shall not apply to elections to be held within a year from the entry into force of such changes. This amendment was designed to prevent last-minute manipulations of Electoral Laws with the purpose of securing additional advantages to the governing parties, a practice with many precedents in the past.

The Law on the Election of Deputies was changed again on 27 October 1995 by Law No. 4125, this time with the intention of reducing disproportionality by enlarging the size of the electoral districts. While in principle each province was considered an electoral district, large provinces that would elect from nineteen to thirty-five deputies would be divided into two districts, and those that would elect thirty-six or more deputies into three districts. Provinces that would elect up to eighteen deputies were considered a single electoral district. Increasing the size of the electoral district is clearly a measure to reduce disproportionality, as alluded to above.

The Law on the Election of Deputies also introduced a change designed to strengthen the representativeness of the legislature. Thus, it was stipulated that, while 450 out of a total of 550 deputies would continue to be elected by the d'Hondt system with double thresholds, 100 deputies would be elected on nationwide party lists without a threshold. However, in another highly controversial ruling in 1995, the Constitutional Court invalidated these provisions, arguing that the constitution permitted the election of deputies from only their specific constituencies. This was based on an erroneous interpretation of Article 80 of the constitution, which stipulated that "deputies shall represent the entire Nation, and not the electoral districts from which they are elected or their voters." Clearly, the objective of this provision was to give the deputies a free representative, rather than a delegate status and, in this sense, it provided no obstacle to their being elected on nationwide lists. In another paradoxical part of the same ruling, the Constitutional Court invalidated the constituency-level thresholds, but found constitutional the 10 percent national threshold.[20] Since then, the Electoral Law has not undergone any other changes.

The Disproportionality of Electoral Systems

Briefly, the *disproportionality of electoral systems* refers to the difference between parties' shares of votes and the percentages of their seats in the legislature. Even though it appears to be a simple concept at first glance, several methods have been proposed for measuring it, such as those by Douglas Rae,[21] John Loosemore and Victor J. Hansby,[22] and Michael Gallagher.[23] In the present study, I use Arend Lijphart's index of disproportionality because of its simplicity. It consists of "the average vote-seat share deviation of the two largest parties in each election. How these large parties fare is a good reflection of the overall proportionality of an election result."[24]

Measuring the proportionality/disproportionality of electoral systems is important not only in comparative research, but also in observing "within-country variations when more than one electoral system is used in the same country; this permits the examination of the effect of changing one aspect of an electoral system while the system remains the same in other respects. Additionally, the effects of small changes *within* electoral systems—changes that are not sufficiently important to signify changes *of* the electoral system—will be examined."[25] This is particularly significant for the Turkish case because different electoral systems have been used and many within-system changes have been made since the beginnings of competitive politics in the country.

If majoritarian systems, which by their very nature produce a high degree of disproportionality, are left aside, it may be more useful to study the problem in proportional representation countries. Several aspects of a proportional system can be identified as having an impact on the party system: the electoral formula (one of the subtypes of proportional representation), constituency magnitude, and electoral thresholds. For countries that do not have a clear legal threshold, one can construct a measure of the effective threshold sensitive to district magnitude.[26]

Table 5.1 shows the disproportionality in elections from 1950 to 2011 according to Lijphart's index. The extremely high level of disproportionality in the 1950–1960 period, when a simple-majority, multimember districts system was in force, and its sudden drop with the adoption of a proportional representation system

Table 5.1 Disproportionality in the Party System, 1950–2011

Election	Percentage of Disproportionality
1950	28.0
1954	32.8
1957	16.7
1961	1.0
1965	0.75
1969	7.4
1973	5.6
1977	5.5
1983	4.5
1987	15.7
1991	7.1
1995	5.8
1999	4.1
2002	22.4
2007	8.0
2011	5.0

in 1961 are entirely expected. Likewise is the drop of disproportionality to its lowest level in the history of Turkish elections in the 1965 election; the only one held under a national remainder version of proportional representation. In the 1969–2011 period, the index varied between 4 and 8, except for two elections: those of 1987 and 2002. In the 1987 election, changes made in the Electoral Law by the ANAP majority prior to the elections gave it a strong advantage, as mentioned above. Consequently, the difference between the ANAP's percentages of votes and of seats was a very large 28.6 percent. In the 2002 election, on the other hand, only two parties (the AKP and CHP) were able to pass the 10 percent national threshold and, therefore, the difference between the AKP's shares of votes and seats was a record-high 31.7 percent. The increase in the district magnitude introduced in 1995 seemed to have had a positive, but limited, effect on disproportionality. Thus, the index fell from 7.1 in 1991 to 5.8 in 1995 and to 4.1 in 1999.

When compared to the twenty-two democracies in Lijphart's study, the Turkish index of disproportionality has been markedly higher under both the majoritarian and the proportional electoral systems. For example, in the United States and the United Kingdom, the average index values for the 1945–1980 period were 5.6 and 6.2, respectively, while they were several times higher than these in Turkey during the 1950–1960 period. Clearly, the differences were due to the fact that in those countries the simple-majority system was used in single-member constituencies whereas in Turkey it was combined with multimember constituencies. Lijphart also observes that the index value for the fifteen countries with a proportional representation system varied from 0.9 (Denmark) to 3.1 (Norway) in the same period[27] while the Turkish figures for the proportional representation period have been much higher. This can be explained mainly by the high national electoral threshold, which obviously increased disproportionately.

Lijphart sees disproportionality "as the hypothesized link between the electoral system variables and the party system variables: the hypothesis is that it is the disproportionality of electoral systems that, by mechanical and psychological means, reduces the number of parties and increases the chances of having majority party victories."[28] Thus, he found meaningful correlations (0.42 and 0.41, respectively) between disproportionality as measured by the least squares index and the frequency of earned parliamentary majorities and of the "manufactured" parliamentary majorities (i.e., those cases where a party obtains a parliamentary majority without a majority of votes) in the fifty-seven proportional representation cases. This hypothesis is borne out not only by the fifty-seven proportional representation systems studied by Lijphart, but also by the Turkish data. Of the nine legislative periods when a party had an absolute majority of seats (those of 1950, 1954, 1957, 1965, 1983, 1987, 2002, 2007, and 2011), only three (those of 1950, 1954, and 1965) were earned majorities and the rest were manufactured ones. In the 2011 elections, the AKP came close to winning an earned majority with 49.8 percent of the votes.

The Choice of an Electoral System

Although electoral systems have strong effects on party systems, it may be argued that the relationship is reciprocal instead of uni-directional. It has been suggested that "precisely because electoral systems may have important consequences on shaping the party system, it can be supposed that they are chosen by already exist-ing political actors in their own interest. Accordingly, it can be expected that, in general, electoral systems will crystallize, con-solidate or reinforce previously existing political party configura-tions, rather than (by themselves) generate new party systems." Thus, in a sense, Duverger's laws are turned "upside down."[29] Indeed, the history of the changes in Turkish Electoral Laws as described above supports this hypothesis since all of these changes were made by the dominant political actors of the time to strengthen their advantages. The ongoing political debates on the question of electoral reform, which I discuss in Chapter 6, provide further evidence of their self-interest-based approach.

Pippa Norris argues in a similar vein that

in the past, electoral systems have usually proved one of the most stable democratic institutions. Minor tinkering with the rules and regulations concerning the administration of elections has been common. . . . Yet until recently wholesale and radical reform of the basic electoral system—meaning the way votes are translated into seats—has been rare. . . . Until recently electoral systems in liberal democracies seemed set in concrete. The parties in government generally favoured and maintained the status quo from which they benefited. The critical voices of those parties or out-groups systematically excluded from elected office rarely proved able to amend the rules of the game.[30]

Norris points out, however, that

in the last decade significant challenges to government legitimacy fuelled the issue of electoral reform. . . . During the 1990s, debate about the electoral system moved from margin to mainstream on the political agenda. This shift produced growing awareness that electoral rules are not neutral: the way votes translate into seats means that some groups, parties, and representatives are ruled into the policy-making process, and some are ruled out. The core debate concerns whether countries should adopt majoritarian systems which prioritize government effectiveness and accountability, or proportional systems which promote greater fairness to minority parties and more diversity in social representation.[31]

It has been shown that this debate is particularly acute in the new democracies of Eastern Europe and Latin America.[32] Since the aims of government effectiveness and accountability on one hand and fairness in representation on the other are contradictory by their very nature, in the final analysis the choice between majoritarian and proportional systems depends on normative preferences, as Lijphart suggests. He asks, "Does one value minority representation and the principle of proportionality more highly than the two-party principle and government accountability, or the other way around?"[33] In divided or segmented societies, however, the choice is much more than a matter of personal normative preferences. In such countries, a proportional system is an essential prerequisite for a stable and functioning democracy.[34]

Notes

1. Maurice Duverger, *Political Parties: Their Organization and Activity in the Modern State* (London: Methuen, 1959), p. 205.
2. Ibid., p. 205.
3. Ibid., p. 217.
4. Ibid., p. 224.
5. Ibid., p. 226.
6. Giovanni Sartori, "The Party Effects of Electoral Systems," in Larry Diamond and Richard Gunther, eds., *Political Parties and Democracy* (Baltimore: Johns Hopkins University Press, 2001), p. 93; emphasis in original. In the same direction, Colin Leys, "Models, Theories, and the Theory of Political Parties," in Harry Eckstein and David Apter, eds., *Comparative Politics: A Reader* (New York: Free Press, 1963), pp. 305–306, 308; William H. Riker, "The Two-Party Systems and Duverger's Law: An Essay on the History of Political Science," *American Political Science Review* 76, no. 4 (1982): 753–766; Josep M. Colomer, "It's Parties That Choose Electoral Systems (or, Duverger's Law Upside Down)," *Political Studies* 53, no. 1 (2005): 1–21. In fact, Duverger admits that "the true effect of the simple-majority system is limited to local bipartism." He qualifies this statement, however, arguing that "the increased centralization of organization within the parties and the consequent tendency to see political problems from the wider, national standpoint tend of themselves to project on to the entire country the localized two-party system brought about by the ballot procedure." Duverger, *Political Parties*, p. 223.
7. Ibid., p. 240.
8. Giovanni Sartori, *Comparative Constitutional Engineering: An Inquiry into Structures, Incentives and Outcomes* (New York: New York University Press, 1994), p. 69.
9. Duverger, *Political Parties*, p. 248.
10. Ibid., pp. 252–253.
11. Erol Tuncer, *Osmanlı'dan Günümüze Seçimler, 1877–1999* (Ankara: TESAV, 2002), pp. 94–109.
12. Ibid., p. 344.
13. Arend Lijphart, *Democracies: Patterns of Majoritarian and Consensus Government in Twenty-one Countries* (New Haven: Yale University Press, 1984), pp. 8, 28, 150–168; the quotation is on p. 150.
14. G. Bingham Powell Jr., *Elections as Instruments of Democracy: Majoritarian and Proportional Visions* (New Haven: Yale University Press, 2000), pp. 4–7.

15. Constitutional Court Decision, E. 1968/15, K. 1968/13, 3, 4, and 5 May 1968, *Anayasa Mahkemesi Kararları Dergisi* (hereafter *AMKD*, Constitutional Court Reports), no. 6, pp. 125–156.

16. Ibid., p. 150.

17. Kenan Evren, *Kenan Evren'in Anıları*, vol. 4 (Istanbul: Milliyet Yayınları, 1991), p. 230.

18. Law No. 3270, 15 April 1986; Law No. 3377, 3 June 1987; Law No. 3403, 11 September 1987; Law No. 3404, 19 October 1987.

19. Constitutional Court Decisions, E. 1987/23, K. 1987/27, 9 October 1987, *AMKD*, no. 23, pp. 380–381; E. 1986/17, K. 1987/11, 22 May 1987, *AMKD*, no. 23, pp. 225–226.

20. Constitutional Court Decision, E. 1995/54, K. 1995/59, 18 November 1995, *Resmî Gazete* (Official Gazette), 21 November 1995, no. 22470, pp. 40, 46–48.

21. Douglas W. Rae, *The Political Consequences of Electoral Laws* (New Haven: Yale University Press, 1967), pp. 84–86.

22. John Loosemore and Victor J. Hanby, "The Theoretical Limits of Maximum Distortion: Some Analytical Expressions for Electoral Systems," *British Journal of Political Science* 1, no. 4 (1971): 467–477.

23. Michael Gallagher, "Proportionality, Disproportionality and Electoral Systems," *Electoral Studies* 10, no. 1 (1991): 33–51.

24. Lijphart, *Democracies,* p. 163. In a more recent study, Lijphart expresses his preference for Gallagher's least squares index. However, he continued to also use his largest deviation index. In his words, "the beauty of this index is that it not only makes good sense but that it is also the simplest possible way of measuring disproportionality." Arend Lijphart, *Electoral Systems and Party Systems: A Study of Twenty-seven Democracies, 1945–1990* (Oxford: Oxford University Press, 1994), pp. 61–62. Ersin Kalaycıoğlu measured disproportionality from 1950 to 2002 according to four indexes. Ersin Kalaycıoğlu, *Turkish Dynamics: Bridge Across Troubled Lands* (New York: Palgrave Macmillan, 2005), p. 92.

25. Lijphart, *Electoral Systems and Party Systems,* p. 7; emphasis in original.

26. Ibid., pp. 25–30; also Rein Taagepera and Matthew S. Shugart, *Seats and Votes: The Effects and Determinants of Electoral Systems* (New Haven: Yale University Press, 1989), pp. 273–275.

27. Lijphart, *Democracies,* p. 160, table 9.1.

28. Lijphart, *Electoral Systems and Party Systems,* pp. 75–77.

29. Colomer, "It's Parties That Choose Electoral Systems," p. 1. See also George E. Lavau, *Parties Politiques et Réalités Sociales: Contribu-*

tion à une Étude Réalistes des Partis Politiques (Paris: Armand Colin, 1953).

30. Pippa Norris, "Choosing Electoral Systems: Proportional, Majoritarian and Mixed Systems," *International Political Science Review* 18, no. 3 (1997): 297–298.

31. Ibid., p. 298.

32. Arend Lijphart and Carlos H. Waisman, eds., *Institutional Design in New Democracies: Eastern Europe and Latin America* (Boulder: Westview Press, 1996), part 1.

33. Lijphart, *Electoral Systems and Party Systems,* p. 144.

34. Lijphart, *Democracies,* p. 28.

6

Current Debates on Electoral Reform

DEBATE ON THE ELECTORAL SYSTEM BEGAN ALMOST AT the start of the multiparty period and has continued to the present. Interestingly, the two radical changes in the electoral system were the products of military interventions, not the outcomes of democratic negotiations and bargainings. The first was the change from a simple-majority system with multimember constituencies to a proportional representation system in the aftermath of the 1960 military coup. As pointed out in Chapter 5, the former system was seen as being responsible for the excessive majority domination during the ousted DP government. The second major change followed the military intervention of 1980. It involved the introduction of a high 10 percent national threshold in addition to constituency thresholds while maintaining the proportional representation system. Other changes made during the periods of civilian governments were essentially marginal changes, as described above (Chapter 5). Perhaps the most consequential among them was the 1995 change in the Electoral Law that enlarged the size of constituencies and thereby reduced the disproportionality in the system. Interestingly, another relatively important change (i.e., the abolition of the constituency thresholds) was the result not of the will of parliament, but of a controversial ruling by the Constitutional Court, as mentioned in Chapter 5.

Throughout this period, majority parties successfully resisted the proposals for electoral system changes that might reduce their advantages. Furthermore, they often changed the rules of the game prior to the elections in order to increase their advantages. To prevent such last-minute electoral manipulations, a provision was added to Article 67 of the constitution to the effect that "changes in electoral laws shall not be applicable to elections to be held within one year from the publication of such laws." However, on several occasions as in 2001 and 2007, parliament got around this provision by adding provisional articles to the constitution, which declared this prohibition inapplicable in the forthcoming elections.

Political Parties' Positions on the Electoral System

During the 1946–1960 period, the electoral system was one of the main points of contestation between the government CHP and the opposition DP. The DP, not expecting to win a parliamentary majority under the simple-majority system with multimember districts,[1] advocated the adoption of a proportional representation system. The CHP, on the other hand, in the belief that the system worked to its advantage, refused such proposals. Thus, the talks between the two parties on this point broke down.[2] However, they agreed on some other aspects of the Electoral Law, such as the introduction of secret balloting, the open counting and sorting of ballots, and a system of judicial review over the electoral process. The new Electoral Law No. 5545, enacted on 16 February 1950, incorporated these changes, and was instrumental in the holding of the May 1950 free elections that resulted in a landslide victory for the DP.

After the change in power in 1950, the two parties radically switched their positions. The DP was no longer an advocate of proportional representation since the majority system was now working in its favor while the minority CHP began to propose a proportional representation system. Thus, a promise for the introduction of proportional representation was included in the CHP's 1957 election platform and its 1959 "Declaration of First Objectives."[3]

The House of Representatives, the civilian wing of the Constituent Assembly established after the 1960 coup, was dominated by the CHP members and sympathizers. The Assembly was entrusted with the task of preparing the new Electoral Laws in addition to a new constitution. As expected, the Assembly enacted into law the CHP's proposal for a proportional representation system for the National Assembly elections. The proportional representation version adopted was the d'Hondt system with constituency thresholds: Law No. 306 on the Election of Deputies of 25 May 1961. Interestingly, however, the CHP majority in the House of Representatives opted for a majoritarian system for the second chamber, the Senate of the Republic: Law No. 304 on the Election of the Members of the Senate of the Republic of 24 May 1961. Probably the choice for a majority system for the second chamber was motivated by the thought that the former DP votes would be divided among the three successor parties (the AP, YTP, and CKMP) and, therefore, the majority system would give a strong majority to the CHP in the Senate. It was hoped that the CHP would retain its weight in the coming political system, regardless of the distribution of seats in the first chamber, the National Assembly.

However, the results of the 1961 Senate elections went completely in the opposite direction, another example of stunning elections. The AP won 47.3 percent of the Senate seats (seventy-one) with 34.5 percent of the votes while the CHP won only 24 percent of the Senate seats (thirty-six) with 36.1 percent of the votes.[4] It appears that the voters of the three successor parties that were competing for the former DP votes strategically concentrated their votes in the strongest competitor to the CHP in their own constituency. Thus, according to Erol Tuncer's calculations, if the National Assembly elections had also been under a majority system, the AP would have gained 216 seats instead of 158 and the CHP 120 seats instead of 173.[5] The expected results of the majority system and the irresistible rise of the AP led parliament to change the electoral system for the Senate to a proportional representation system with constituency thresholds on 17 April

1994 (Law No. 447) and then to adopt a national remainder system for both chambers on 13 February 1965 (Law No. 533).

As explained in Chapter 5, even the adoption of a national remainder system could not prevent the AP from winning a majority of the National Assembly seats in the 1965 elections. The AP, in turn, in order to solidify its majority position, attempted to change the electoral system once again in 1968 from the national remainder system to a d'Hondt system with constituency thresholds for both chambers. However, the Constitutional Court annulled the provisions of the law relating to constituency thresholds. Therefore, the system remained as a d'Hondt system without thresholds until the military intervention of 1980.

The double-threshold system introduced by the military regime of 1980–1983 clearly favored the strongest party (the ANAP from 1983 to 1991). Thus, it won an absolute majority of the seats with much less than a majority of votes in the 1983 and 1987 parliamentary elections. Understandably, the ANAP was unenthusiastic about proposals to change the system in a more proportional direction. On the contrary, it introduced certain changes in the system in 1986 and 1987 to strengthen the majoritarian character of the system, as discussed in Chapter 5. Throughout this period, the opposition parties advocated a more proportional system.

A symposium organized by the think tank the Turkish Social, Economic, and Political Research Foundation (TESAV) on 12 November 1994 provides useful information on the position of parties in the electoral system. In this symposium, the ANAP (which had already lost its majority in the 1991 elections) and the DYP advocated a single-member majority system with two ballots, according to which the two candidates with the most votes would contest the second ballot. However, the second ballot would take place in larger constituencies that would partially permit proportional representation.[6] The details of this curious mixture were never explained. The other parties (the CHP, MHP, SHP, DSP) advocated a proportional system with a lower national threshold, such as 4 percent or 5 percent, and objected to both single-member constituencies and a double ballot.[7]

Although the 1991 elections brought to power a DYP-SHP coalition, few of these proposals found a place in the Election

Law adopted on 27 October 1995 (Law No. 4125). The major change introduced by the new law was to increase the size of the constituencies in order to reduce the disproportionality in the system. On the other hand, the law did not change either the national or the constituency threshold. However, the Constitutional Court invalidated the constituency threshold while leaving the national threshold intact in its ruling, discussed in Chapter 5. The court also invalidated the provisions permitting the elections of 100 (out of 550) deputies on national party lists according to a proportional representation system without a threshold.

Since 1995, there has been no change in the electoral system and the debates have concentrated essentially on the national threshold. Expectedly, minor parties have proposed either the total abolition of the national threshold or lowering it to a more reasonable level such as 5 percent.[8] Again as expected, the AKP, which is highly overrepresented by the present national threshold system, does not agree with such proposals. The main opposition party, CHP, did not initially raise this issue since it also benefited from the present system. Thus, in the 2002 elections, in which only two parties passed the 10 percent national threshold, it won 32.4 percent of the seats with 19.4 percent of the votes. More recently, however, the CHP has advocated the lowering of the national threshold to around 5 percent.

The conformity of the national threshold to the European human rights standards has been the subject of a case before the European Court of Human Rights. The applicants were Mehmet Yumak and Resul Sadak, who failed to get elected in the 2002 elections, even though their party (the DEHAP) list obtained 45.05 percent of the votes in the Kurdish-majority province of Şırnak. The applicants claimed that this constituted a violation of Article 3 of Protocol No. 1 (the right to free elections) to the European Convention of Human Rights (ECHR). The Grand Chamber of the court decided, however, that there was no violation of the convention. The court observed that "the national 10% threshold was the highest of all the thresholds applied in the member States of the Council of Europe" and stated that it "attached importance to the views of the Council of Europe bodies which agreed that the level of the Turkish national threshold was exceptionally high and had called for it to be lowered." The court concluded, however, that "it was not persuaded that . . . the impugned 10% threshold had had the effect of impairing the essence of the applicants' rights under Article 3 of Protocol No. 1." In the court's view, "the variety of situations provided for in the member states' electoral legislation illustrated the diversity of the possible options. . . . Any electoral system must be assessed in the light of the country's political evolution."[9]

Individual Proposals for Electoral Reform

In the period under study (1961 to the present), a number of scholars and experts have proposed different reform strategies. Hikmet Sami Türk's proposal, put forward in 1976, for example, consists of modifying the d'Hondt system in a less proportional direction. In the classical d'Hondt system, the numbers of votes obtained by parties are divided by 1, 2, 3, and so on, and then the figures obtained are ordered from the highest to the lowest and the seats are allocated accordingly. Türk proposes to start the division with 1.5 instead of 1 and to continue dividing by half-digit figures such as 1.5, 2, and 2.5. This is, in a sense, the opposite of the Sainte-Laguë system (using the odd-integer divisor series 1, 3, 5, 7, etc., in order to increase proportionality), and it aims at giving a greater advantage to major parties in order to facilitate governability at the expense of proportionality.[10] Thus, if this system had been applied in the 1969 elections the AP would have won 313 seats instead of 256, and in the 1977 elections the CHP would have won 227 seats instead of 213.[11]

In a study sponsored by the Turkish Association of Industrialists and Businessmen (TÜSİAD), a leading businessmen's association, Seyfettin Gürsel proposes a single-member double-ballot majority system for 500 deputies and proportional representation on nationwide party lists for 50 seats. He argues that such a system would allow centrist parties to win an absolute majority of seats with a much lower percentage of votes and encourage center-right, center-left, and center-right/center-left coalitions. He also argues that a double-ballot system would have a centrifugal drive and, therefore, would contribute to both political stability and social peace.[12] Apparently, one purpose behind this and similar proposals is to limit the parliamentary representation of the allegedly antisystem parties, such as the rapidly rising pro-Islamist RP, thereby making it easier for the formation of centrist coalitions.

In a study again sponsored by TÜSİAD, Murat Sertel and Ersin Kalaycıoğlu make a proposal with a similar aim but a different mechanism: a "majoritarian compromise" formula. This system is somewhat similar to the Australian alternative vote system, according to which voters would also indicate their second, third, and so on, choices on their ballots. Sertel and Kalaycıoğlu argue that this system could be combined with either single-member or multimember constituencies. In the former case, if no party obtains a majority of the first choices, then the second, third, and so on, choices would be distributed until a candidate obtains a majority.[13] If it had been adopted, this system would also have had the effect of limiting the parliamentary representation of the antisystem parties since it would be unlikely that such parties would be the second or third choice of a majority of voters.

Proposals for more modest changes in the electoral system include lowering the national threshold to 5 percent, allowing parties to form electoral coalitions and to present joint lists, introducing preferential voting, and electing 100 deputies from national party lists according to a proportional representation system.[14]

Public Opinion and Issues of Electoral Reform

A large-scale survey sponsored by TÜSİAD provides interesting data about public attitudes toward issues of electoral reform.[15] A majority of the respondents (65 percent) believed that a change in the electoral system is an important dimension of democratization. Another 86.5 percent of the respondents complained that, because electoral districts are too large, voters do not have a chance of becoming informed about the candidates. A similar majority (84.8 percent) thought that even unpopular candidates could be elected on party lists, 80.5 percent believed that major parties do not take seriously the demands of minor party voters since minority parties have no chance of passing the national threshold, and 79.8 percent said that the high national threshold weakens trust in the electoral system. Along the same lines, 77.9 percent believed that the system allows certain parties to be represented in parliament out of proportion to their actual strength. However, a majority (71.9 percent) thought that coalition governments are not successful.[16]

Another interesting finding of the TÜSİAD study is that a majority of the respondents prioritized governability and government stability over fairness in representation. Thus, according to two-thirds (66.6 percent) of the respondents, the principal function of an electoral system should be to facilitate the formation of a stable government. Similarly, 55.2 percent were against a system with too many parties. With regard to the 10 percent national threshold, public opinion seems to be divided: 39.6 percent were in favor of maintaining it as is, 24.7 percent for increasing it, 12.1 percent for lowering it, and 24.1 percent for abolishing it completely. Two-thirds of the respondents (67.1 percent) were against the proposal of electing a portion of deputies from nationwide party lists. Public opinion was also divided with regard to the double-ballot system: 51.0 percent in favor and 43.0 percent against. Similarly, single-member constituencies were supported by 43.0 percent while 52.1 percent were against it.[17]

Conclusion

The findings of the studies described above indicate a good deal of confusion and inconsistency in the minds of voters. Thus, even though a majority expressed a desire to know the candidates better, there was no majority support for a single-member system that would best satisfy this need. Likewise, although a majority thought that the present system allows certain parties to be represented in parliament out of proportion to their strength, only a minority favored lowering or abolishing the national threshold—the principal cause of such disproportionality.

Realistically speaking, some version of proportional representation has been used since 1961, and there seems to be little likelihood of changing the system in a majoritarian direction. Indeed, Article 67 of the constitution, which stipulates that electoral laws should reconcile the principles of stability in government and fairness in representation, is an obstacle to the adoption of a purely majoritarian system. However, this formula allows parliament to choose a mixed system, in which a certain proportion of deputies would be elected by a proportional representation system and others by a single-member majority system.

The single-member majority system has both supporters and opponents in Turkey. The opponents argue that, in addition to its potential of producing extremely disproportionate results, such a system would encourage patron-client relations and personalistic influences, aggravate ethnic and sectarian divisions, and involve deputies in local issues and constituency services at the expense of national issues. Furthermore, in a country with a high rate of population growth and internal migration, it would require the redrawing of electoral district boundaries before almost every election.[18]

On the other hand, proponents of the single-member system argue that such a system would strengthen the ties between voters and deputies, thereby weakening the excessively strict party discipline, because deputies would owe their position to local popularity rather than loyalty to the party and its leader. However, this is a mixed blessing. Contemporary democracy is, by and large, party democracy. Most voters do not vote on the basis of the personal characteristics of candidates, but on the program and policies of the party to which they belong. Weak party discipline would preclude the development of responsible party government and governmental accountability in elections. The liberal theories of representation that see deputies as free agents who would vote only in accordance with their individual conscience have given way to more collectivist theories of representation.[19]

In conclusion, what seems to be at issue now is not a system change, but a change within the proportional representation system. As expected, all minor parties and the main opposition party (the CHP) are in favor of either abolishing the national threshold or lowering it to a more acceptable level such as 5 percent. However, since the present majority party (the AKP) is the chief beneficiary of the national threshold and strongly opposed to abolishing it, there is almost no likelihood of such a change. On the other hand, the AKP spokepersons occasionally express their support for a mixed system in which 100 of 550 deputies would be elected on party lists according to proportional representation without a threshold. Recall that such a system was introduced by the Electoral Law of 1995, but was invalidated by the Constitutional Court (Chapter 5).

The most objectionable aspect of the high national threshold is that it heavily penalizes regional, in particular Kurdish, ethnic parties whose popular support is concentrated in the Kurdish-majority southeastern region. For example, in the 2002 parliamentary elections in Diyarbakır Province, the DEHAP did not win any seats with 56 percent of the vote while the AKP won eight seats with 16 percent and the CHP two seats with only 5.9 percent of the vote. In Hakkari Province, the DEHAP won no seats with 45 percent of the vote while the CHP and the AKP each won one with 8 percent and 7 percent, respectively. In Batman Province, the DEHAP won no seats with 47 percent of the vote, but the AKP won three seats with 20.6 percent and the CHP one seat with 7 percent. In Şırnak Province, the DEHAP won no seats with 46 percent of the vote while the AKP won two seats with 14 percent and the CHP one seat with 4.7 percent. In the 2007 and 2011 parliamentary elections, the successor Kurdish parties overcame this obstacle by presenting their candidates as independents and were able to send deputies to parliament. However, this method involves serious organizational difficulties for such parties and probably results in their underrepresentation. One possible way out of this dilemma would be to maintain the national threshold, but not apply it to parties that obtain a plurality of votes in a certain number of constituencies, as is done in the cases of Germany, Sweden, and Denmark.[20]

Although it is not directly related to the electoral system, a frequently debated issue regarding the electoral process is the excessive central control over the nomination of parliamentary candidates. Under Article 37 of the Law on Political Parties, parties are allowed to nominate their parliamentary candidates in any way determined by their party constitutions. The practice in recent decades in all major parties has been to have all or most candidates chosen by their central executive bodies. Only if those bodies decide to hold party primaries to choose candidates in some or all of the constituencies (a rare occurrence), such primaries are to be held in accordance with the detailed provisions of the Law on Political Parties on the basis of a free, equal, and secret vote by all registered party members and under the supervision of official electoral boards (Articles 37–52). To make this system obligatory for all parties, as some critics suggest, would amount to an unjust interference in the internal processes of political parties.

The present system of nominations has been criticized as leading to excessive leadership control over the process and, consequently, to hierarchical party structures and strict party discipline in parliamentary voting. Although such criticism contains a great deal of truth, it would be a mistake to hold only the electoral and the nomination systems responsible for such an outcome. Strong party leadership and hierarchical party structures are also the result of certain deep-rooted characteristics of Turkish political culture, and they have remained an almost constant feature of Turkish party politics under different electoral and nomination systems.

Conversely, certain changes in the electoral system may reduce such strong leadership domination and strict party discipline. The most radical of such changes would be the adoption of a single-member simple-plurality system. However, this system would present certain disadvantages as discussed above and, at present, there is no strong demand for such a radical change. The introduction of some variant of preferential voting would also be somewhat helpful in this regard. However, when this system was in force from the 1980s until it was abolished in 1995, it did not seem to create an appreciable difference. Thus, it appears that strong party leadership and strict discipline are likely to remain major features of Turkish political parties in the foreseeable future.

Notes

1. Celal Bayar, then leader of the DP, stated in an interview in *Tercüman* (Istanbul daily) many years later that "we were expecting to come

to power, but we were not expecting such a big majority. . . . Indeed, I had not thought about such a big victory." Quoted in Tanel Demirel, *Türkiye'nin Uzun On Yılı: Demokrat Parti İktidarı ve 27 Mayıs Darbesi* (Istanbul: İstanbul Bilgi Üniversitesi Yayınları, 2011), p. 103, n. 25.

2. Ibid., pp. 66–67.

3. Ibid., pp. 197, 226. See also Metin Toker, *Demokrasimizin İsmet Paşa'lı Yılları: DP'nin Altın Yılları, 1950–1954* (Ankara: Bilgi Yayınevi, 1991), p. 24.

4. Erol Tuncer, *Osmanlı'dan Günümüze Seçimler, 1877–1999* (Ankara: TESAV, 2002), p. 344.

5. Erol Tuncer, "Çok Partili Dönemde Seçim Uygulamaları," in Hikmet Sami Türk and Erol Tuncer, eds., *Türkiye İçin Nasıl Bir Seçim Sistemi: Sistem Önerileri, Seçim Uygulamaları* (Ankara: TESAV, 1995), p. 91.

6. Hikmet Sami Türk and Erol Tuncer, *Türkiye İçin Nasıl Bir Seçim Sistemi: Sistem Önerileri, Seçim Uygulamaları* (Ankara: TESAV, 1995), pp. 155, 194.

7. Ibid., pp. 174–175, 188, 199, 216–217.

8. On the views of political parties expressed in a symposium organized by TESAV on 18–19 February 2005, see TESAV, *Siyasi Partiler ve Seçim Kanunlarında Değişiklik Önerileri* (Ankara: TESAV, 2005), pp. 185–249.

9. Grand Chamber Judgement, *Yumak and Sadak v. Turkey*, Application No. 10226/03, 21 November 2007. For an analysis of this decision, see Ergun Özbudun, *Türkiye'nin Anayasa Krizi* (Ankara: Liberte Yayınları, 2009), pp. 18–21.

10. Hikmet Sami Türk, "Türkiye İçin Nasıl Bir Seçim Sistemi," in Helmet Sami Türk and Erol Tuncer, eds., *Türkiye İçin Nasıl Bir Seçim Sistemi: Sistem Önerileri, Seçim Uygulamaları* (Ankara: TESAV, 1995), pp. 30–36. See also Hikmet Sami Türk, *Seçim Hukukunun Temel Sorunları ve Çözüm Önerileri* (Ankara: TESAV, 1997).

11. Tuncer, "Çok Partili Dönemde Seçim Uygulamaları," pp. 93–96.

12. Seyfettin Gürsel, *Siyasal İstikrar ve İki Turlu Dar Bölge Seçim Sistemi Simülasyon Modeli* (Istanbul: TÜSİAD, 1998).

13. Murat Sertel and Ersin Kalaycıoğlu, *Türkiye İçin Yeni Bir Seçim Yöntemi Tasarımına Doğru* (Istanbul: TÜSİAD, 1995), esp. pp. 65–73, 109–118.

14. For example, Işın Çelebi, *Siyasi Partiler ve Seçim Kanunları Önerisi* (N.p., 2007), pp. 164–167.

15. TÜSİAD, *Seçim Sistemi ve Siyasi Partiler Araştırması*, vol. 1: *Temel Bulgu ve Sonuçlar* (Istanbul: TÜSİAD, November 2001).

16. Ibid., pp. 55–66.

17. TÜSİAD, *Seçim Sistemi ve Siyasi Partiler Araştırması*, vol. 2, pp. 129–180.

18. Türk, "Türkiye İçin Nasıl Bir Seçim Sistemi," pp. 10–14.

19. Samuel H. Beer, *British Politics in the Collectivist Age* (New York: Alfred A. Knopf, 1965); Ergun Özbudun, *Party Cohesion in Western Democracies: A Causal Analysis,* Sage Professional Papers in Comparative Politics (Beverly Hills, CA: Sage, 1970), pp. 363–379.

20. Özbudun, *Türkiye'nin Anayasa Krizi*, pp. 20–21.

Bibliography

Ahmad, Feroz. *The Turkish Experiment in Democracy, 1950–1975* (Boulder: Westview Press, 1977).

———. *The Young Turks: The Committee of Union and Progress in Turkish Politics, 1908–14* (Oxford: Clarendon, 1969).

Akarlı, Engin Deniz. "The State as a Socio-cultural Phenomenon and Political Participation in Turkey," in Engin D. Akarlı with Gabriel Ben-Dor, eds., *Political Participation in Turkey: Historical Background and Present Problems* (Istanbul: Boğaziçi University, 1975), pp. 135–155.

Akın, Rıdvan. *TBMM Devleti* (Istanbul: İletişim, 2001).

Akşin, Sina. "İttihat ve Terakki Üzerine," *AÜ Siyasal Bilgiler Fakültesi Dergisi* 26, no. 2 (1971): 153–182.

———. *Jön Türkler ve İttihat ve Terakki* (Istanbul: Gerçek Yayınevi, 1980).

Akyol, Taha. *Atatürk'ün İhtilal Hukuku* (Istanbul: Doğan Kitap, 2012).

Anderson, Perry. *Lineages of the Absolutist State* (London: Verso, 1979).

Atatürk'ün Söylev ve Demeçleri II, 1906–1938 (Ankara: Türk Tarih Kurumu Basımevi, 1959).

Ateş, Nevin Yurtsever. *Türkiye Cumhuriyetinin Kuruluşu ve Terakkiperver Cumhuriyet Fırkası* (Istanbul: Sarmal Yayınevi, 1994).

Ayata, Ayşe. "The Emergence of Identity Politics in Turkey," *New Perspectives on Turkey* 17, no. 3 (1997): 59–73.

————. "Ideology, Social Bases, and Organizational Structure of the Post-1980 Political Parties," in Atilla Eralp, Muharrem Tünay, and Birol Yeşilada, eds., *The Political and Socioeconomic Transformation of Turkey* (Westport, CT: Praeger, 1983), pp. 31–49.

Ayata, Ayşe Güneş, and Sencer Ayata. "Ethnic and Religious Bases of Voting," in Sabri Sayarı and Yılmaz Esmer, eds., *Politics, Parties and Elections in Turkey* (Boulder: Lynne Rienner, 2002), pp. 137–155.

Bartolini, Stefano, and Peter Mair. *Identity, Competition and Electoral Availability: The Stabilization of European Electorates, 1885–1985* (Cambridge: Cambridge University Press, 1990).

Bayramoğlu, Ali. *28 Şubat: Bir Müdahalenin Güncesi* (Istanbul: Birey Yayınları, 2001).

Beer, Samuel H. *British Politics in the Collectivist Age* (New York: Alfred A. Knopf, 1965).

Belge, Ceren. "Friends of the Court: The Republican Alliance and Selective Activism of the Constitutional Court in Turkey," *Law and Society Review* 40, no. 3 (2006): 653–691.

Belge, Murat. *Militarist Modernleşme: Almanya, Japonya ve Türkiye* (Istanbul: İletişim, 2011).

Bianchi, Robert. *Interest Groups and Political Development in Turkey* (Princeton, NJ: Princeton University Press, 1984).

Blondel, Jean. "Party Systems and Patterns of Government in Western Democracies," *Canadian Journal of Political Science* 1, no. 2 (1968): 180–203.

Burçak, Rıfkı Salim. *Türkiye'de Demokrasiye Geçiş, 1945–1950* (Olgaç Yayınevi, 1979).

Burnham, Walter Dean. *Critical Elections and the Mainsprings of American Politics* (New York: Norton, 1970).

Çandar, Cengiz. "PKK Olayı bir Kürt İsyanıdır," *Taraf* (Istanbul daily), 27 June 2011.

Çarkoğlu, Ali. "Ideology or Economic Pragmatism? Profiling Turkish Voters in 2007," *Turkish Studies* 9, no. 2 (2008): 317–344.

————. "The Nature of Left-Right Ideological Self-Placement in the Turkish Context," *Turkish Studies* 8, no. 2 (2007): 253–271.

————. "The Turkish Party System in Transition: Party Performance and Agenda Change," *Political Studies* 46, no. 3 (1998): 544–571.

Çarkoğlu, Ali, and Melvin J. Hinich, "A Spatial Analysis of Turkish Party Preferences," *Electoral Studies*, 25, no. 2 (2006): 369–392.

Çarkoğlu, Ali, and Ersin Kalaycıoğlu. *The Rising Tide of Conservatism in Turkey* (New York: Palgrave Macmillan, 2009).

Çarkoğlu, Ali, and Binnaz Toprak. *Değişen Türkiye'de Din, Toplum ve Siyaset* (Istanbul: TESEV, 2006).

Cebesoy, Ali Fuat. *Siyasi Hâtıralar,* vol. 2 (Istanbul: Doğan Kardeş Yayınları, 1960).

Çelebi, Işın. *Siyasi Partiler ve Seçim Kanunları Önerisi* (N.p., 2007).

Çınar, Alev, and Burak Arıkan. "The Nationalist Action Party: Representing the State, the Nation, or the Nationalists?" in Barry Rubin and Metin Heper, eds., *Political Parties in Turkey* (London: Frank Cass, 2002), pp. 25–40.

Çınar, Menderes. "The Justice and Development Party and the Kemalist Establishment," in Ümit Cizre, ed., *Secular and Islamic Politics in Turkey* (London: Routledge, 2008), pp. 109–131.

Çoker, Fahri. *Türk Parlâmento Tarihi, Millî Mücadele ve TBMM Birinci Dönem* (Ankara: TBMM, 1995).

Colomer, Josep M. "It's Parties That Choose Electoral System (or, Duverger's Law Upside Down)," *Political Studies* 53, no. 1 (2005): 1–21.

Crewe, Ivor. "Introduction: Electoral Change in Western Democracies: A Framework for Analysis," in Ivor Crewe and David Denver, eds., *Electoral Change in Western Democracies: Patterns and Sources of Electoral Volatility* (London: Croom Helm, 1985), pp. 1–22.

Dağı, İhsan. *Turkey Between Democracy and Militarism: Post Kemalist Perspectives* (Ankara: Orion, 2008).

Demirel, Ahmet. *Birinci Mecliste Muhalefet* (Istanbul: İletişim, 2009).

Demirel, Tanel. *Türkiye'nin Uzun On Yılı: Demokrat Parti İktidarı ve 27 Mayıs Darbesi* (Istanbul: İstanbul Bilgi Üniversitesi Yayınları, 2011).

Devereux, Robert. *The First Ottoman Constitutional Period: A Study of the Midhat Constitution and Parliament* (Baltimore, MD: Johns Hopkins University Press, 1963).

Duverger, Maurice. *Political Parties: Their Organization and Activity in the Modern State* (London: Methuen, 1959).

Ecevit, Bülent. *Atatürk ve Devrimcilik* (Ankara: 1971).

Ergüder, Üstün. "The Motherland Party, 1983–1989," in Metin Heper and Jacob M. Landau, eds., *Political Parties and Democracy in Turkey* (London: I. B. Tauris, 1991), pp. 152–169.

Ergüder, Üstün, and Richard Hofferbert. "The 1983 General Election in Turkey: Continuity or Change in Voting Patterns?" in Metin Heper and Ahmet Evin, eds., *State, Democracy, and Military: Turkey in the 1980s* (Berlin: de Gruyter, 1988), pp. 81–102.

Ersson, Svante, and Jan-Erik Lane. "Democratic Party Systems in Europe: Dimensions, Change and Stability," *Scandinavian Political Studies* 5, no. 1 (1982): 67–96.

Esmer, Yılmaz. "At the Ballot Box: Determinants of Voting Behavior," in Sabri Sayarı and Yılmaz Esmer, eds., *Politics, Parties and Elections in Turkey* (Boulder: Lynne Rienner, 2002), pp. 91–114.

————. *2007 Milletvekili Genel Seçimleri Seçmen Davranışı ve Tercihleri Seçim Sonrası Araştırması* (mimeo).

Evren, Kenan. *Kenan Evren'in Anıları,* vol. 4 (Istanbul: Milliyet Yayınları, 1991).

Finefrock, Michael M. "The Second Group in the First Grand National Assembly," *Journal of South Asia and Middle Eastern Studies* 3, no. 1 (1979): 3–17.

Flanagan, Scott C., and Russell J. Dalton. "Parties Under Stress: Realignment and Dealignment in Advanced Industrial Societies," *West European Politics* 7, no. 1 (1984): 7–23.

Frey, Frederick W. "Patterns of Elite Politics in Turkey," in George Lenczowski, ed., *Political Elites in the Middle East* (Washington, DC: American Enterprise Institute for Public Policy Research, 1975), pp. 41–82.

————. "Themes in Contemporary Turkish Politics," Massachusetts Institute of Technology, 1970 (mimeo).

————. *The Turkish Political Elite* (Cambridge: MIT Press, 1965).

Gallagher, Michael. "Proportionality, Disproportionality and Electoral Systems," *Electoral Studies* 10, no. 1 (1991): 33–51.

Gibb, H. A. R., and Harold Bowen. *Islamic Society and the West,* vol. 1 (London: Oxford University Press, 1950).

Gologlu, Mahmut. *Demokrasiye Geçiş, 1946–1950* (Istanbul: Kaynak Yayınları, 1982).

————. *Üçüncü Meşrutiyet, 1920* (Ankara: Başnur Matbaası, 1971).

Görmüş, Alper. "Yüzde 20 Seçimden Ümidini Kesti mi?" *Taraf* (Istanbul daily), 8 July 2011.

Güneş, İhsan. *Birinci Türkiye Büyük Millet Meclisinin Düşünsel Yapısı, 1920–1921* (Eskişehir, Turkey: Anadolu Üniversitesi Yayını, 1985).

Güney, Aylin. "The People's Democracy Party," in Barry Rubin and Metin Heper, eds., *Political Parties in Turkey* (London: Frank Cass, 2002), pp. 122–137.

Gürsel, Seyfettin. *Siyasal İstikrar ve İki Turlu Dar Bölge Seçim Sistemi Simülasyon Modeli* (Istanbul: TÜSİAD, 1998).

Hale, William, and Ergun Özbudun. *Islamism, Democracy and Liberalism in Turkey: The Case of the AKP* (London: Routledge, 2010).

Hanioğlu, Şükrü. *Preparation for a Revolution: The Young Turks, 1902–1908* (New York: Oxford University Press, 2000).

Hazama, Yasushi. *Electoral Volatility in Turkey: Cleavages vs. the Economy* (Chiba, Japan: Institute of Developing Economies, 2007).

———. "Social Cleavages and Electoral Support in Turkey: Toward Convergence," *The Developing Economies* 41, no. 3 (2003): 362–387.

Heper, Metin. *The State Tradition in Turkey* (Walkington, UK: Eothen Press, 1985).

———, ed. *Strong State and Economic Interest Groups: The Post-1980 Turkish Experience* (Berlin: de Gruyter, 1991).

Hermet, Guy, Richard Rose, and Alain Rouquié, eds. *Elections Without Choice* (New York: Wiley, 1978).

Hirschman, Albert O. "Social Conflicts as Pillars of Democratic Market Society," *Political Theory* 22, no. 2 (1994): 203–218.

Hourani, Albert. "Ottoman Reform and the Politics of Notables," in William R. Polk and Richard L. Chambers, eds., *Beginnings of Modernization in the Middle East: The Nineteenth Century* (Chicago: University of Chicago Press, 1968), pp. 41–68.

Huntington, Samuel P. "Social and Institutional Dynamics of One-Party Systems," in Samuel P. Huntington and Clement H. Moore, eds., *Authoritarian Politics in Modern Society: The Dynamics of Established One-Party Systems* (New York: Basic Books, 1970), pp. 3–47.

———. *The Third Wave: Democratization in the Late Twentieth Century* (Norman: University of Oklahoma Press, 1991).

İnalcık, Halil. "The Nature of Traditional Society: Turkey," in Robert E. Ward and Dankwart A. Rustow, eds., *Political Modernization in Japan and Turkey* (Princeton, NJ: Princeton University Press, 1964), pp. 42–63.

———. "The Ottoman Economic Mind and Aspects of the Ottoman Economy," in M. A. Cook, ed., *Studies in the Economic History of the Middle East from the Rise of Islam to the Present Day* (London: Oxford University Press, 1970), pp. 207–218.

Inglehart, Ronald. "The Changing Structure of Political Cleavages in Western Society," in Russell J. Dalton, Scott C. Flanagan, and Paul Allen Beck, eds., *Electoral Change in Advanced Industrial Democracies: Realignment or Dealignment?* (Princeton, NJ: Princeton University Press, 1984), pp. 25–69.

———. *The Silent Revolution: Changing Values and Political Styles Among Western Publics* (Princeton, NJ: Princeton University Press, 1977).

İnsel, Ahmet. "The AKP and Normalizing Democracy in Turkey," *South Atlantic Quarterly* 102, nos. 2–3 (2003): 293–308.

Kalaycıoğlu, Ersin. "Elections and Party Preferences in Turkey: Changes and Continuities in the 1990s," *Comparative Political Studies* 27, no. 4 (1994): 402–424.

————. "Justice and Development Party at the Helm: Resurgence of Islam or Restitution of the Right-of-Center Predominant Party?" *Turkish Studies* 11, no. 1 (2010): 29–44.

————. "The Motherland Party: The Challenge of Institutionalization in a Charismatic Leader Party," in Barry Rubin and Metin Heper, eds., *Political Parties in Turkey* (London: Frank Cass, 2002), pp. 41–61.

————. "The Shaping of Party Preferences in Turkey: Coping with the Post–Cold War Era," *New Perspectives on Turkey* 20, no. 1 (1999): 47–76.

————. *Turkish Dynamics: Bridge Across Troubled Lands* (New York: Palgrave Macmillan, 2005).

Karpat, Kemal H. "The Transformation of the Ottoman State, 1789–1908," *International Journal of Middle East Studies* 3, no. 3 (1972): 243–281.

————. *Turkey's Politics: The Transition to a Multi-Party System* (Princeton, NJ: Princeton University Press, 1959).

Key, V. O., Jr. "Secular Realignment and the Party System," *Journal of Politics* 21, no. 2 (1959): 198–210.

————. "A Theory of Critical Elections," *Journal of Politics* 17, no. 1 (1955): 3–18.

Koçak, Cemil. *Birinci Meclis* (Istanbul: Sabancı Üniversitesi, 1998).

Kongar, Emre. *Türkiye'nin Toplumsal Yapısı,* vol. 1 (Istanbul: Remzi Kitabevi, 1985).

KONDA. *Seçim'07: Siyasal Eğilimler Araştırmaları Özet Rapor* (18 July 2007).

KONDA Araştırma. *Kürt Mesele'sinde Algı ve Beklentiler* (Istanbul: İletişim, 2011).

Küçükömer, İdris. *Düzenin Yabancılaşması: Batılaşma* (Istanbul: Ant Yayınları, n.d.).

Laakso, Markku, and Rein Taagepera. "Effective Number of Parties: A Measure with Application to West Europe," *Comparative Political Studies* 12, no. 1 (1979): 3–27.

Landau, Jacob M. *Radical Politics in Modern Turkey* (Leiden: E. J. Brill, 1974).

La Palombara, Joseph, and Myron Weiner. "The Origin and Development of Political Parties," in Joseph La Palombara and Myron

Weiner, eds., *Political Parties and Political Development* (Princeton, NJ: Princeton University Press, 1966), pp. 3–42.

Lavau, George E. *Parties Politiques et Réalités Sociales: Contribution à une Étude Réalistes des Partis Politiques* (Paris: Armand Colin, 1953).

Lerner, Hanna. "Constitution-Writing in Deeply Divided Societies: The Incrementalist Approach," *Nations and Nationalism* 16, no. 1 (2010): 68–88.

Lewis, Bernard. *The Emergence of Modern Turkey* (London: Oxford University Press, 1966).

Leys, Colin. "Models, Theories, and the Theory of Political Parties," in Harry Eckstein and David Apter, eds., *Comparative Politics: A Reader* (New York: Free Press, 1963), pp. 305–315.

Lijphart, Arend. *Democracies: Patterns of Majoritarian and Consensus Government in Twenty-one Countries* (New Haven, CT: Yale University Press, 1984).

———. *Electoral Systems and Party Systems: A Study of Twenty-seven Democracies, 1945–1990* (Oxford: Oxford University Press, 1994).

Lijphart, Arend, and Carlos H. Waisman, eds. *Institutional Design in New Democracies: Eastern Europe and Latin America* (Boulder, CO: Westview Press, 1996).

Linz, Juan J. *The Breakdown of Democratic Regimes: Crisis, Breakdown, and Reequilibration* (Baltimore, MD: Johns Hopkins University Press, 1978).

Lipset, Seymour Martin, and Stein Rokkan. "Cleavage Structures, Party Systems, and Voter Alignments: An Introduction," in Seymour Martin Lipset and Stein Rokkan, eds., *Party Systems and Voter Alignments: Cross-National Perspectives* (NewYork: Free Press, 1967), pp. 1–64.

Loosemore, John, and Victor J. Hanby. "The Theoretical Limits of Maximum Distortion: Some Analytical Expressions for Electoral Systems," *British Journal of Political Science* 1, no. 4 (1971): 467–477.

Mainwaring, Scott P. "Party Systems in the Third Wave," *Journal of Democracy* 9, no. 3 (1998): 67–81.

Mainwaring, Scott, and Edurne Zoco. "Political Sequences and Stabilization of Interparty Competition: Electoral Volatility in Old and New Democracies," *Party Politics* 13, no. 2 (2007): 155–178.

Mair, Peter. *Party System Change: Approaches and Interpretations* (Oxford: Clarendon Press, 1997).

Mardin, Şerif. "Center-Periphery Relations: A Key to Turkish Politics?" *Dædalus* 2, no. 1 (1973): 169–190.

————. *The Genesis of Young Ottoman Thought: A Study in the Modernization of Turkish Political Ideas* (Princeton, NJ: Princeton University Press, 1962).

————. "Historical Determinants of Social Stratification: Social Class and Class Consciousness in Turkey," *A.Ü. Siyasal Bilgiler Fakültesi Dergisi* 22, no. 4 (1967): 111–142.

Morlino, Leonardo. "Political Parties and Democratic Consolidation in Southern Europe," in Richard Gunther, P. Nikiforos Diamandouros, and Hans-Jürgen Puhle, eds., *The Politics of Democratic Consolidation: Southern Europe in Comparative Perspective* (Baltimore, MD: Johns Hopkins University Press, 1995), pp. 315–388.

Norris, Pippa. "Choosing Electoral Systems: Proportional, Majoritarian and Mixed Systems," *International Political Science Review* 18, no. 3 (1997): 297–298.

O'Donnell, Guillermo. "Delegative Democracy," *Journal of Democracy* 5, no. 1 (1994): 55–69.

Öniş, Ziya. "Conservative Globalists Versus Defensive Nationalists: Political Parties and Paradoxes of Europeanization in Turkey," *Journal of Southern Europe and the Balkans* 9, no. 3 (2007): 247–260.

————. "Globalization, Democratization and the Far Right: Turkey's Nationalist Action Party in Critical Perspective," *Democratization* 10, no. 1 (2003): 27–52.

————. "The Political Economy of Turkey's Justice and Development Party," in M. Hakan Yavuz, ed., *The Emergence of a New Turkey: Democracy and the AK Parti* (Salt Lake City: University of Utah Press, 2006), pp. 207–234.

Öz, Esat. *Otoriterizm ve Siyaset: Türkiye'de Tek-Parti Rejimi ve Siyasal Katılma, 1923–1945* (Ankara: Yetkin Yayınevi, 1996).

Özbudun, Ergun. "Changes and Continuities in the Turkish Party System," *Representation* 42, no. 2 (2006): 129–137.

————. *The Constitutional System of Turkey: 1876 to the Present* (New York: Palgrave Macmillan, 2011).

————. *Contemporary Turkish Politics: Challenges to Democratic Consolidation* (Boulder: Lynne Rienner, 2000).

————. "Established Revolution Versus Unfinished Revolution: Contrasting Patterns of Democratization in Mexico and Turkey," in Samuel P. Huntington and Clement H. Moore, eds., *Authoritarian Politics in Modern Society: The Dynamics of Established One-Party Systems* (New York: Basic Books, 1970), pp. 380–405.

————. "Income Distribution as an Issue in Turkish Politics," in Ergun Özbudun and Aydın Ulusan, eds., *The Political Economy of Income*

Distribution in Turkey (New York: Holmes & Meier, 1980), pp. 55–82.

———. "The Nature of the Kemalist Political Regime," in Ali Kazancıgil and Ergun Özbudun, eds., *Atatürk: Founder of a Modern State*, 2nd ed. (London: C. Hurst, 1997), pp. 79–102.

———. *1921 Anayasası* (Ankara: Atatürk Araştırma Merkezi, 1992).

———. *Otoriter Rejimler, Seçimsel Demokrasiler ve Türkiye* (Istanbul: Bilgi Üniversitesi Yayınları, 2011).

———. "The Ottoman Legacy and the Middle East State Tradition," in L. Carl Brown, ed., *Imperial Legacy: The Ottoman Imprint on the Balkans and the Middle East* (New York: Columbia University Press, 1996), pp. 133–157.

———. *Party Cohesion in Western Democracies: A Causal Analysis*, Sage Professional Papers in Comparative Politics (Beverly Hills, CA: Sage, 1970).

———. *Social Change and Political Participation in Turkey* (Princeton, NJ: Princeton University Press, 1976).

———. "Turkey," in Myron Weiner and Ergun Özbudun, eds., *Competitive Elections in Developing Countries* (Durham, NC: Duke University Press; American Enterprise Institute, 1987), pp. 328–365.

———. "Turkey: Plural Society and Monolithic State," in Ahmet T. Kuru and Alfred Stepan, eds., *Democracy, Islam, and Secularism in Turkey* (New York: Columbia University Press, 2012), pp. 61–94.

———. "The Turkish Party System: Institutionalization, Polarization and Fragmentation," *Middle Eastern Studies* 17, no. 2 (1981): 228–240.

———. *Türkiye'nin Anayasa Krizi* (Ankara: Liberte Yayınları, 2009).

———. "Why the Crisis over the Presidency?" *Private View* 12 (2007): 48–51.

Özbudun, Ergun, and Ömer Faruk Gençkaya. *Democratization and the Politics of Constitution-Making in Turkey* (Budapest: Central European University Press, 2009).

Özbudun, Ergun, and Frank Tachau. "Social Change and Electoral Behavior in Turkey: Towards a 'Critical Realignment'?" *International Journal of Middle East Studies* 6, no. 4 (1975): 460–480.

Parla, Taha. *Türkiye'de Siyasal Kültürün Resmî Kaynakları*, 3 vols. (Istanbul: İletişim, 1991, 1992).

Parla, Taha, and Andrew Davison. *Corporatist Ideology in Kemalist Turkey: Progress or Order?* (Syracuse, NY: Syracuse University Press, 2004).

Pedersen, Mogens N. "The Dynamics of European Party Systems: Changing Patterns of Electoral Volatility," *European Journal of Political Research* 7, no. 1 (1979): 1–26.

Powell, G. Bingham, Jr. *Elections as Instruments of Democracy: Majoritarian and Proportional Visions* (New Haven, CT: Yale University Press, 2000).

Rae, Douglas W. *The Political Consequences of Electoral Laws* (New Haven, CT: Yale University Press, 1967).

Riker, William H. "The Two-Party Systems and Duverger's Law: An Essay on the History of Political Science," *American Political Science Review* 76, no. 4 (1982): 753–766.

Rose, Richard, and D. W. Urwin. "Persistence and Change in Western Party Systems Since 1945," *Political Studies* 18, no. 3 (1970): 287–319.

Rustow, Dankwart A. "Atatürk as Founder of a State," in *Prof. Dr. Yavuz Abadan'a Armağan* (Ankara: AÜSBF Yayını, 1969), pp. 517–573.

———. "The Military: Turkey," in Robert E. Ward and Dankwart A. Rustow, eds., *Political Modernization in Japan and Turkey* (Princeton, NJ: Princeton University Press, 1964), pp. 352–388.

Sartori, Giovanni. *Comparative Constitutional Engineering: An Inquiry into Structures, Incentives and Outcomes* (New York: New York University Press, 1994).

———. *Parties and Party Systems: A Framework for Analysis* (Cambridge: Cambridge University Press, 1976).

———. "The Party Effects of Electoral Systems," in Larry Diamond and Richard Gunther, eds., *Political Parties and Democracy* (Baltimore, MD: Johns Hopkins University Press, 2001), pp. 90–105.

Sayarı, Sabri. "The Changing Party System," in Sabri Sayarı and Yılmaz Esmer, eds., *Politics, Parties and Elections in Turkey* (Boulder: Lynne Rienner, 2002), pp. 9–32.

Sertel, Murat, and Ersin Kalaycıoğlu. *Türkiye İçin Yeni Bir Seçim Yöntemi Tasarımına Doğru* (Istanbul: TÜSİAD, 1995).

Sezgin, Ömür. *Türk Kurtuluş Savaşı ve Siyasal Rejim Sorunu* (Ankara: Birey ve Toplum Yayıncılık, 1984).

Shamir, Michal. "Are Western Party Systems 'Frozen'?: A Comparative Dynamic Analysis," *Comparative Political Studies* 17, no. 1 (1984): 35–79.

Smith, Elaine Diana. *Turkey: Origins of the Kemalist Movement and Government of the Grand National Assembly* (Washington, DC: Judd & Detweiler, 1959).

Sunar, İlkay. *State, Society and Democracy in Turkey* (Istanbul: Bahçeşehir University, n.d.).

―――. *State and Society in the Politics of Turkey's Development* (Ankara: A.Ü. Siyasal Bilgiler Fakültesi Yayını, 1974).

Sunar, İlkay, and Sabri Sayarı. "Democracy in Turkey: Problems and Prospects," in Guillermo O'Donnell, Philippe C. Schmitter, and Lawrence Whitehead, eds., *Transitions from Authoritarian-Rule: Southern Europe* (Baltimore, MD: Johns Hopkins University Press, 1986), pp. 165–186.

Taagepera, Rein, and Matthew S. Shugart. *Seats and Votes: The Effects and Determinants of Electoral Systems* (New Haven, CT: Yale University Press, 1989).

TESAV. *Siyasi Partiler ve Seçim Kanunlarında Değişiklik Önerileri* (Ankara: TESAV, 2005).

Toker, Metin. *Demokrasimizin İsmet Paşa'lı Yılları: Demokrasiden Darbeye, 1957–1960* (Ankara: Bilgi Yayınevi, 1991).

―――. *Demokrasimizin İsmet Paşa'lı Yılları: DP'nin Altın Yılları, 1950–1954* (Ankara: Bilgi Yayınevi, 1991).

―――. *Demokrasimizin İsmet Paşa'lı Yılları: Tek Partiden Çok Partiye, 1944–1950* (Ankara: Bilgi Yayınevi, 1990).

Tunaya, Tarık Zafer. *Türkiye'de Siyasal Partiler,* vol. 1: *İkinci Meşrutiyet Dönemi, 1908–1918* (Istanbul: Hürriyet Vakfı Yayınları, 1984).

Tunçay, Mete. *Türkiye Cumhuriyetinde Tek-Parti Sisteminin Kurulması, 1923–1931* (Ankara: Yurt Yayınları, 1981).

Tuncer, Erol. "Çok partili Dönemde Seçim Uygulamaları," in Hikmet Sami Türk and Erol Tuncer, eds., *Türkiye İçin Nasıl Bir Seçim Sistemi: Sistem Önerileri, Seçim Uygulamaları* (Ankara: TESAV, 1995), pp. 47–122.

―――. *1950 Seçimleri* (Ankara: TESAV, 2010).

―――. *Osmanlı'dan Günümüze Seçimler, 1877–1999* (Ankara: TESAV, 2002).

―――. *Seçim 2011: 12 Haziran 2011 Milletvekili Genel Seçimleri, Sayısal ve Siyasal Değerlendirme* (Ankara: TESAV, 2011).

Türk, Hikmet Sami. *Seçim Hukukunun Temel Sorunları ve Çözüm Önerileri* (Ankara: TESAV, 1997).

―――. "Türkiye İçin Nasıl Bir Seçim Sistemi," in Hikmet Sami Türk and Erol Tuncer, eds., *Türkiye İçin Nasıl Bir Seçim Sistemi: Sistem Önerileri, Seçim Uygulamaları* (Ankara: TESAV, 1995), pp. 1–43.

Türk, Hikmet Sami, and Erol Tuncer. *Türkiye İçin Nasıl Bir Seçim Sistemi: Sistem Önerileri, Seçim Uygulamaları* (Ankara: TESAV, 1995).

TÜSİAD. *Seçim Sistemi ve Siyasi Partiler Araştırması,* vol. 1: *Temel Bulgu ve Sonuçlar* (Istanbul: TÜSİAD, November 2001).

Wuthrich, F. Michael. "Paradigms and Dynamic Change in the Turkish Party System" (PhD dissertation, Bilkent University, 2011).

Yavuz, M. Hakan. "Introduction: The Role of the New Bourgeoisie in the Transformation of the Turkish Islamic Movement," in M. Hakan Yavuz, ed., *The Emergence of a New Turkey: Democracy and the AK Parti* (Salt Lake City: University of Utah Press, 2006), pp. 1–19.

Yetkin, Çetin. *Türkiye'de Tek-Parti Yönetimi, 1930–1945* (Istanbul: Altın Kitaplar, 1983).

Yılmaz, Hakan. "Democratization from Above in Response to the International Context: Turkey, 1945–1950," *New Perspectives on Turkey* 17 (Fall 1997): 1–38.

Yücekök, Ahmet N. *Siyaset Sosyolojisi Açısından Türkiye'de Parlamentonun Evrimi* (Ankara: A.Ü. Siyasal Bilgiler Fakültesi Yayını, 1983).

Zürcher, Erik J. *Political Opposition in the Early Turkish Republic: The Progressive Republican Party, 1924–1925* (Leiden: E. J. Brill, 1991).

———. *Turkey: A Modern History* (London: I. B. Tauris, 1994), pp. 70–71.

———. *The Unionist Factor: The Role of the Committee of Union and Progress in the Turkish National Movement* (Leiden: E. J. Brill, 1984).

Index

149

About the Book

DESPITE RADICAL CHANGES IN TURKISH POLITICS SINCE the transition to a multiparty system in the mid-1940s, the center-right parties have consistently won an electoral majority. Why? How have they managed to maintain such a firm hold in the face of social cleavages that pit modernizing, secularist state elites against a conservative and pious majority? Ergun Özbudun uses the lens of Turkey's party and electoral systems to enhance our understanding of the country's polarized politics.

Ergun Özbudun is professor of political science and constitutional law at Istanbul Şehir University. His publications include *Social Change and Political Participation in Turkey* and *Contemporary Turkish Politics: Challenges to Democratic Consolidation.*